101 Ways to Help Preschoolers Excel in Reading, Writing, and Speaking

Catherine DePino

Rowman & Littlefield Education
Lanham, Maryland • Toronto • Plymouth, UK

Published in the United States of America
by Rowman & Littlefield Education
A Division of Rowman & Littlefield Publishers, Inc.
A wholly owned subsidary of The Rowman & Littlefield Publishing Group, Inc.
4501 Forbes Boulevard, Suite 200, Lanham, Maryland 20706
www.rowmaneducation.com

Estover Road
Plymouth PL6 7PY
United Kingdom

British Library Cataloguing in Publication Information Available

Library of Congress Cataloging-in-Publication Data

DePino, Catherine.
  101 ways to help preschoolers excel in reading, writing, and speaking / Catherine
DePino.
    p. cm.
  ISBN-13: 978-1-57886-559-8 (hardback : alk. paper)
  ISBN-10: 1-57886-559-X (hardback : alk. paper)
  ISBN-13: 978-1-57886-575-8 (pbk. : alk. paper)
  ISBN-10: 1-57886-575-1 (pbk. : alk. paper)
  1. Language arts (Preschool) 2. Education, Preschool—Activity programs. I. Title.
II. Title: One hundred one ways to help preschoolers excel in reading, writing, and
speaking. III. Title: One hundred and one ways to help preschoolers excel in reading,
writing, and speaking.
LB1140.5.L3D46 2007
372.6—dc22   2006036668

To my dear daughter,
Melissa DePino Cooper, a caring, creative, and
enterprising businesswoman.

She walks in beauty, like the night
Of cloudless climes and starry skies. . . .
—Lord Byron

CONTENTS

Contents

PART II: ACTIVITIES AGES 4–6

Contents

ACKNOWLEDGMENTS

Thanks to Dr. Tom Koerner, always the gentleman, for his constant encouragement and kindness, and to Paul Cacciato for his professionalism and guidance. Thanks also to Erin McGarvey for her pleasant manner and assistance in the production process.

HOW TO USE THIS BOOK

This book gives preschoolers valuable practice in reading, writing, and speaking skills by engaging them in a series of enjoyable activities. Preschool teachers, nursery and day care workers, kindergarten teachers, parents (especially home-schooling parents), and ESL teachers will find the activities both easy to follow and user-friendly.

Use your own creativity to adjust the activities to a child's ability and maturity levels. You can make modifications such as having the child *say* instead of write responses or use gestures and pantomime. For children who are learning to write, you can use invented spelling and write the correct spelling underneath the words.

Invented spelling is "an attempt by beginning writers to spell a word when the standard spelling is unknown." It involves using "whatever knowledge of sounds or visual patterns the writer has" (Bank Street College). Proponents of invented spelling believe that using it helps students express themselves in writing at an earlier age and does not hamper their ability to spell as they progress in their writing development. If you have strong objections to using invented spelling, the child can dictate writing to the teacher or homework helper.

When you use the activities dealing with parts of speech (nouns, verbs, adjectives, adverbs), feel free to use the simpler terms (*naming words*, *actions words*, or *words that describe*) or the standard terms, whichever best serves your students.

You can use the activities with groups in a classroom setting as well as with individual children in a home setting. In the home, you can encourage siblings and extended family members to participate in the activities. For example, when the instructions tell the children to take turns with each other, a family member can take the place of a peer. Similarly, if the activity calls for student partners to work together, the child can pair up with a parent, sibling, or other family member.

All of the activities address values important to children's growth and development: cooperation, friendship, respect for others' opinions, intergenerational closeness, generosity, and gratitude.

Every child has a primary learning style: auditory (learns through hearing), visual (learns through seeing), or kinesthetic (learns through touch and movement).

If you watch a child play and interact with family, friends, and classmates, it will help you determine if the child learns best by hearing, seeing, or touching and moving. Through your observations, you may decide that the child has a combination of learning styles.

The activities in this book address all three learning styles. If you find that a child learns best by using one learning style, try adjusting an activity to accommodate it. For example, if the child learns mainly through touch and movement, you can add more hands-on activities like drawing, coloring, writing, and using the computer. If the child is a visual learner, use more visuals, things he or she can see, such as pictures with vivid colors and books with striking illustrations. If a child learns best by hearing, add more listening and speaking components, such as conversations, audiotapes, and music.

The activities are divided into two main sections: early preschoolers (ages 2–4) and preschoolers (ages 4–6). Within each of these categories, activities progress from basic to intermediate to advanced. You can modify or expand upon all of the activities, adjusting them to a child's individual needs.

The activities begin with a description of what you will accomplish during the activity. *Target Skills* tell you at a glance which skills the activity reinforces. *Things You'll Need* tells you which materials you need to assemble ahead of time to prepare for the activity.

The *Game Plan* gives a step-by-step chronological list of what to do from the activity's beginning to end. *Sample Scripts* help you talk to children about the activities appearing throughout the book. Take as long as you need to complete each activity. You can work with many of the activities over a period of several days.

Many of the activities involve homework helpers: parents, guardians, siblings, or other family members. You will find a notation that an activity requires a homework helper next to the name of the activity. Copying and sending home (via a communications envelope) the entire lesson will ensure successful implementation of the activity. Send instructions home with the children well in advance of the activity so that the homework helper can ask questions that arise.

The homework helper's involvement reinforces the concepts you're teaching and creates a bond between the helper, you, and the child as a learning team and as a powerful force to create lifelong learners.

"You can teach any child any subject at any age in an intellectually responsible way."

—Jerome Bruner

PART I
ACTIVITIES
AGES 2-4

BASIC

1. One, Two, I Love You

Description: Reinforce verbal, counting, and memory skills and build creativity by using rhyme. Help the child tell a rhyming story using primary numbers.

Target Skills: Speaking, vocabulary development, storytelling, and awareness of rhyme in poetry

Things You'll Need: Prewritten simple rhymes using numbers

Game Plan

1. Before starting the activity, make up a few simple rhymes using numbers from one to ten. Rhymes may rhyme within the same line or at the end of the line.

2. Stop at the end of the line or wherever the rhyming word belongs. See if the children can fill in the missing rhyming word with the one you thought of or with an original word. Give a small prize for every appropriate rhyme a child gives.

3. Children will work with partners to write a number poem of two lines, using any numbers they choose from one to fifty. They will tell their poems to the class.

Sample Script: "I'm going to make up a rhyme about numbers from one to ten. See if you can fill in the rhyming word when I stop reading. If you want, you can think of your own word as long as it rhymes. The rhyme may be in the middle or at the end of the line. Here's an example: (Stop where you want the child to fill in the rhyming word.)

> One, *two*, I love *you*.
> Three *four*, eat some *more*.
> Five *six*, New York *Knicks*.
> Seven *eight*, sorry I'm *late*.
> Nine *ten*, let's count *again*.

"Can you think of your own number rhyme? Work with a partner to think of a two-line rhyming poem. Put the numbers in order, and use any numbers from one to fifty. You can use one or more numbers in each line. Make your poem rhyme in the middle or at the end of the line. Tomorrow you will tell your poem to the class."

2. Paint a Story

Description: Enhance creative and storytelling powers using finger paint to create mood.

Target Skills: Writing, reading, speaking, listening, and organizational skills

Things You'll Need: Picture storybook with a simple plot, finger paint, and heavy-duty paper

Game Plan

1. Gather supplies and tell the children you're going to read them a story. After you read the story, ask them to paint a picture showing what the story is about.

2. Ask the students to take turns telling you the story in their own words. Ask them to tell about their favorite parts of the story. Have them identify the beginning, middle, and end of the story.

3. Have the children paint their own stories (total of three pages) with a different page for each part of the story, beginning, middle, and end.

4. After the children complete the three paintings (you may want to have them work on the picture stories on three consecutive days), have them number the pages.

5. Ask students to tell their stories to the class and point to the pictures that show the beginning, middle, and end of the story. Ask why they chose certain colors for their characters' clothes and setting.

6. Bind the stories into a book and display them.

7. As a follow-up, children will paint stories at home. The homework helper will read them a story of their choice, which they will depict in a drawing. Before painting their stories, they will work with their homework helpers to figure out the beginning, middle, and end to the stories. The children will tell their stories to the helpers and other family members.

Sample Script: "I'm going to tell you a story. You can tell the same story with paints and paper. After we talk about the story, draw the people in the story doing something you heard me read about. Paint the place where the story happens, and paint three pictures. Paint one picture for the beginning, one for the middle, and one for the end of the story. It's a good idea to plan a story before you paint. That's what writers do before they write a story. After you finish your painting, you will tell the class the story in your own words.

"Next, you're going to paint another story with your homework helper. After your homework helper reads the story, talk about what happens before you start painting your story. After you finish your story, tell it to your helper and other family members."

3. Flaky Fish in a Fancy Dish

Description: Teach descriptive skills and speaking skills, and make creative comparisons about foods using rhymes and comparisons with *like* or *as*.

Target Skills: Writing (making creative comparisons using similes) and speaking

Things You'll Need: Foods a child eats regularly (or children can think of foods they've eaten)

Game Plan

1. Bring in foods the children are familiar with and have them describe the tastes, textures, and colors of the various foods.

2. Have them compare the color to something else they've seen. Orange carrots are the same color as a harvest moon or pumpkin; a purple plum may look like a toy kangaroo; and a red tomato may be the color of a tulip or a red ball. Take turns naming foods and objects of the same color.

3. You can also make up simple rhymes (*flaky fish in a fancy dish*, for example) to describe foods the children eat at home.

4. Invite the children to create a two-word rhyme by combining the name of a food with another rhyming word. The rhyming word can create a humorous effect and can be a regular or nonsense word that doesn't need to relate to the food (see Sample Script).

5. For a final activity, encourage the children to create comparison sentences comparing foods with common objects. They will use the words *like* or *as* to make their comparisons: "The chocolate ice cream is as brown as a cow," or "The pizza is as red as my jacket."

6. Write the children's sentences on the board. Read them to the class and ask which two things are compared in the sentences.

Sample Script: "Let's play a matching color game with food. We'll take turns. I'll name a food, and you show me something here that's the same color. Then *you* name a food and ask me to tell you something that's the same color.

"We'll take turns until we run out of things to compare. For example: What do you see at home or in school that's the same color as milk?" (Possible answers: *my cat, the snow outside,* or *the clouds*). "What do you see outside that is the same color as peas?" (Possible answer: the grass and the tree outside the kitchen window.)

"Next, I'd like you to think of two-word rhymes to tell about foods you've eaten. The rhymes can be real words or funny words that rhyme (peas, please; apple, bapple; cake, snake; juice, moose; jelly, belly; cheese, sneeze).

"For our next game, I'd like you think of longer rhymes to describe foods you've eaten at home or in a restaurant: for example, *mellow vanilla yogurt*; *lean, green string beans*; and *flaky fish in a fancy dish*.

"The last thing you'll do is tell me comparison sentences using the words *like* or *as*. Here are two comparison sentences using colors: 'The night sky is as purple as a queen's robe,' or 'The full moon looks like a big, white beach ball.' I'd like you to tell me which two things are being compared in the sentences after I read the examples that the class tells me."

4. A World Awash in Color (Homework Helper Activity)

Description: Build memory skills and ability to recreate a natural wonder (trees, flowers, or leaves, for example) with pictures and/or words.

Target Skills: Writing (description), speaking, and memory skills

Things You'll Need: Crayons (large box with many colors), white paper, and books with nature pictures

Game Plan

1. Find books in the library that have large, colorful pictures of nature scenes. Look at the books with the children and ask them to name the colors of trees and flowers and to describe changes the different seasons bring.

2. If the children live in a climate different from some of the pictures in the books (no snow or no warm weather, for example), ask them to compare what they see with their own climate. Ask what they think it would be like to live in a different climate. How would they feel physically? How would their

clothes be different? What kinds of things could they do in a different climate that they couldn't do where they live? Ask where they would rather live and why.

3. Within a day or two of your discussion, take a nature walk with the children. Point out the variety of colors: the deep green of an evergreen tree, the pink and orange sun, or the red, orange, and gold fall leaves. Ask them to describe the colors they see.

4. Take brief notes or make a chart about what the class tells you (examples: *tree*: dark green; *sky*: light blue with white clouds; *tulips*: bright red and yellow; and *birds*: blue, red, and brown). Point out the names of other colors in nature with which they may not be familiar (salmon, turquoise, fuchsia, and mustard yellow).

5. When you return from the walk, have the children name the different things they saw and the colors they identified (use the notes you took as a reminder).

6. Ask the children to choose crayons that look the same as the colors of the sights they remember seeing in nature. Have them draw three to four pictures (one to a page) of some of the sights they saw. Put the pictures in an envelope for them to take home to their homework helpers.

7. The homework helpers will help the children label their pictures with the names of the natural wonders and their colors and make up a cover for the booklets. The helpers will bind the booklets using a ribbon or staples.

8. The children will bring their completed booklets to school. They will explain to the class what they drew and name the colors of each natural scene.

Sample Script: "Let's look at these books and see how many different colors we can find in nature. Tomorrow we'll go for a walk outside and look for the same colors we saw in the books. Then we're going to make our own books about colors in nature.

"You'll draw one picture on each page and draw three or four pictures of something we saw on our walk. Find the crayon color that looks most like what you saw, and use that color for your picture.

"Here are some pictures you might want to draw: leaves of many colors falling from trees; the yellow sun beating down on a blue green lake; a bed of pink and red roses; or mounds of white snow coating the ground under a clear blue sky.

"After you finish your pictures, you'll take them home. Your homework helper will write the names of the things you drew on your pictures as you say them. They will also write the names of the colors you used for each picture on your drawing. When you finish drawing the pictures, your helper will help you make a cover for the book, and you'll give your story a name.

"You'll bring your book to school next week and show everyone your pictures and tell them about the beautiful sights you saw in nature."

5. Hidden Treasures Everywhere (Homework Helper Activity)

Description: Enhance powers of observation and description and storytelling skills by going on a treasure hunt in the neighborhood, on the beach, or in the mountains.

Target Skills: Writing (storytelling), speaking, describing, and making choices

Things You'll Need: Gift bags for collecting treasures (If the treasure hunt takes place at a family vacation spot, the child will bring plastic pails and shovels.)

Game Plan

1. Before you start out on your walk, tell the children they'll be searching for treasures—objects left behind by nature, or by people who were in this place before. Tell them to collect only those things that attract them.

9

2. One child may find a seashell that makes a roaring sound like the ocean when held to the ear or a beach toy that lay buried in the sand. If you're walking in the park, the child may spot a rock that when cleaned and polished looks like a precious gem, or a shiny penny that has dropped unnoticed from someone's pocket.

3. As the children pick up objects and decide to keep or return them, they will begin to think about which objects attract them and hold meaning for them. They are also learning to make choices. Point out that although they may not find a particular object interesting, it may be someone else's treasure. One child may pop a red plastic ring into a pail without hesitation, while another child would prefer a piece of seaweed to decorate a sand castle.

4. As the children choose items for their collection, encourage them to describe them using descriptive adjectives (words that describe).

5. After the children have collected and described a couple of items, ask them to use the adjectives to help them make up a story about the objects. If you tell a story about some objects you've found, you'll help them learn how to tell their own stories. Make your story short and simple, and let your imagination guide you. Model descriptive sentences such as: "I see a purple shell. It's the color of the sky at nighttime" or "Doesn't this pink shell look like an elephant's ear?" If a child doesn't speak in sentences, he or she can use simple descriptive words or phrases that describe color (*pink*), size (*tiny*), or shape (*circle*).

6. When you return from the treasure hunt, have the class clean and polish their treasures. Have the children bring in a special case or container to store their treasures. They and a homework helper can cover a shoebox with pretty wrapping paper and decorate it with stickers and glitter or find a colorful plastic container in the dollar store.

7. Ask the children to tell the class the most important treasure they found on their treasure hunt and to make up a brief story about it. Encourage the children to show family members their discoveries and to tell them stories about the objects.

Sample Script: "Today we're going to look for hidden treasures in the neighborhood. When you look at different objects you'd like to bring back to class, think of what you'll call the objects (pretty shell or sparkly ring, for example). Think of words to describe the objects. Use these words to help you make up a story about the treasures you found.

"If you choose a shell, you might say, 'A small fish once lived in this shell deep in the ocean with its family. It left the shell behind so that people would remember that a fish once lived there. The shell will last a long, long time and will make everyone who sees it happy.'

"After we come back from our treasure hunt, you'll clean and polish your treasures and put them in a special container that you've decorated with your homework helper. Then you'll tell everyone the name of your favorite treasure and tell a story about it. After that, you'll share your treasure and your story with your family."

Pretty Please and Thank You

Description: Promote courteous behavior and practice knowing what to say in social situations. Build writing skills by writing courteous notes to family and friends.

Target Skills: Speaking, writing, and character development (courteous behavior)

Things You'll Need: Thank-you notes (bought or homemade), computer greeting card with message space (free on the Internet), and prewritten index cards to play a courtesy game (see #4, Game Plan).

Game Plan

1. Let the children catch you thanking someone (another child, a family member) for things you sometimes take for granted such as putting toys away without being asked.

2. Model polite behavior by speaking to others (children, staff, family) with respect as if they were close friends. In line with this, talk to the children about specific ways of making another person's day special.

3. Give the children ideas about doing something kind for others. Have the class give their own ideas. For example, draw a picture, roll it up, and tie it with a bow, give it to a relative or friend; help straighten out a room; call an older relative; send a thank-you note after someone gives a gift or shows kindness; or make a pretty card to cheer someone up (either draw it on construction paper with markers and glitter, or create it on the computer by logging on to one of the companies that offers free cards).

4. You can also play "What would you say if . . . ," another activity that encourages courtesy. Think up social situations that require the children to use polite words such as *please, thank you,* or *excuse me.* Write the situations on index cards and have the children choose cards. Ask them to think of polite expressions to use in each situation. To simplify the activity, you can write response cards for each situation and have the children choose appropriate responses from the prewritten cards.

Sample Script: "Can you tell me about when you heard someone at home or school thank someone for doing something helpful to them? Why was thanking them a good thing?" (Sample answers: It made them feel they did something good. It made them want to help more.)

"What can you do to help another child in the class?" (Suggestions: I can help Jeff tie his shoes, or Sara looks like she's all alone—I can ask her if she wants to color with me.)

"What can you do to help at home?" (Suggestions: I can help my parents by setting the table, or I can call my grandparents to see how they are.)

"After a school or family trip, you can say, 'Let's write the restaurant manager a thank-you card for showing us how to make ice cream.' What did you like best about going to the restaurant? You make up the words for the card, and I'll help you write it. Stick on the stamp and you can mail it.

"Today we're going to play a game about courtesy called 'What would you say if.'" Choose one of these cards. Here are some of the questions on the cards and some answers you might give: "What would you say if you wanted a cold drink?" (Sample answer: May I please have some juice?) "What would you say if you accidentally stepped on someone's toe?" (Sample answer: Sorry. Are you okay?) "What would you say if a friend gave you a book for your birthday?" (Thanks. I can't wait to read it.) "What would you say if you interrupted someone who was talking?" (Sample answer: Excuse me.) "Now you pick a card and tell me what you would say."

7. Uncle Oscar Has a Shiny, Bald Head (Homework Helper Activity)

Description: Show the child who's who in the family photo album and help him or her learn to associate pictures with people. Practice writing skills by creating a poem for a family member.

Target Skills: Writing, speaking, and memory skills

Things You'll Need: Photographs of family members

Game Plan

1. The next time a family member visits the home, the parent can ask the relative to tell the child a brief story about his or her childhood. The parent can ask the relative to bring a childhood picture to show the child how he or she looked then and now. The child can share the picture with the class and tell about the relative.

2. The children bring in one or more pictures of family members. Ask the children to point out identifying physical characteristics such as Uncle Oscar's shiny, bald head or Aunt Meg's curly, white hair. Have them tell something about the relative's personality that makes that person one of a kind. (Examples: Uncle Oscar has three sheepdogs and makes cakes from scratch; Aunt Meg drives a motorcycle and paints houses.)

3. After the visit, the homework helper can help the child write a short free verse poem about the person. This kind of poem is called free verse because it doesn't rhyme. The child will draw a picture of the person doing something that he or she is famous for.

4. The child will show the family member's picture to the class, and the teacher will read the poem that the child and homework helper wrote.

Sample Script: "You and your homework helper are going to write a poem about one of your family members. First, your relative will talk to you about when he or she was growing up and will show you pictures. You'll talk with your homework helper about what you want to write. Think of some interesting things you can write in the poem. What does your family member look like? What does he or she like to do?"

Example of free verse poem for a family member:

> Uncle Oscar doesn't have much hair,
> but he has bright blue eyes.
> He takes his three sheepdogs
> wherever he goes,
> except when he rides his motorcycle.
> He makes chocolate cakes from scratch.
> That's the best thing
> about Uncle Oscar.

"Bring in the picture your family member gave you or one you drew, and tell the class about your relative. I'll read the poem that you wrote with your homework helper."

 8. Jam Session (Homework Helper Activity)

Description: Jump-start creativity and listening skills by encouraging the child to make and play homemade musical instruments.

Target Skills: Speaking and listening

Things You'll Need: A cardboard paper towel roll for each child to make a toy flute, saucepans of varying sizes, drums made with boxes or pots and pans, wooden spoons and flatware spoons, scissors (for you), and blunt scissors if the child can cut with them.

Game Plan

1. Have the children bring paper towel rolls into class on an assigned day. Set out different sized pots and containers with varying surfaces, widths, and components (plastic, metal), along with wooden and flatware spoons.

2. Model each of the activities for the children. Have them make familiar sounds (animal sounds, etc.) on their flutes by using the opening at the end of the flute. The children can try to guess the sounds their classmates make with their instruments.

3. Ask them to sing the melody of familiar songs (nursery rhymes such as "London Bridge" or popular songs) into the towel roll. They can also re-create the melody by singing the piece of music with the word *do* sung repeatedly instead of singing the lyrics. The children can take turns guessing each other's song titles.

4. The children can also use the towel roll as a karaoke microphone and sing into the large opening at the top to amplify their voices. They can stage a karaoke show with the class or with family members.

5. Line up pots, pans, and spoons in order of size. Have the children experiment with different combinations of pans and spoons. Ask which sounds they like most and why. They can also play along to recorded music with the drums. Ask them to write original songs using their drums and/or flutes and to play their songs for family members and the class.

15

Sample Script: "You will bring a paper towel roll to class to use as a flute.

"I'd like you to try making different types of sounds into the opening at one end of your flute. Make sounds you've heard before such as animals, a siren, or a car horn. You'll try to guess sounds the other children make, and they can guess which sounds you're making.

"Next you're going to take turns singing into your towel roll flute. Instead of singing the words, you can sing the word *do* to the melody of your song." (Demonstrate this for the class.)

"You can also use the towel roll as a karaoke microphone and sing into it to make your voice louder. Try giving a karaoke show at home and let us know how it turned out. Tell us about the song you sang and sing it here if you want.

"As our final activity, we'll play the drums (pans, plastic containers, or toy drums or a combination). Tell me how the drums sound different when you use the wooden spoons instead of the plastic ones or metal ones. Which sound do you like best and why?

"Next, I'm going to play (or sing) a song. Would you like to play along on your drums? Now you can try writing your own song (with or without words) using the horns and or drums. Practice at home with your helper and then play it for your family and us."

9. How Many Ways Can a Bubble Be? (Homework Helper Activity)

Description: Reinforce critical thinking and verbal skills through creative play with bubbles. Demonstrate cause and effect. Help the child write a free verse poem describing bubble adventures.

Target Skills: Speaking, writing, descriptive skills, critical thinking, making comparisons, and learning about cause and effect

Things You'll Need: Soap bubbles and different types of bubble pipes and wands

Game Plan

1. When you blow bubbles with the children, consider cause and effect. Ask how changing the way they blow bubbles changes the shape and size of the bubbles. Talk about how the bubbles will look different if the children stand still, spin around, jump, or wave the wand gently or forcefully.

2. Ask them to take turns describing how the bubbles look when they connect small bubbles to build one big one versus when they create individual bubbles.

3. Ask the homework helpers to have the children tell them a story about making different types of bubbles. Ask them to write the story as the child dictates it. The children will illustrate their stories by drawing and coloring the different types of bubbles.

4. After blowing bubbles in class, write a simple free verse poem with the children (large group activity) about the different sizes, shapes, and colors of bubbles. Focus on comparisons when writing about bubbles.

Sample Script: "Let's try blowing different kinds of bubbles. Tell me about the different kinds of bubbles you can make with the same wand. How do the bubbles from the pipe look different from the bubbles from the wand? How do they look when you blow them through the wand and when you wave the wand in the air? What colors can you see in the bubbles?

"Let's look at the bubbles when we make one big bubble and compare it to when we make a lot of little bubbles and connect them. Tell me how the bubbles look different.

"Your homework helper will help you write a story about the different types of bubbles we made. You tell the story and the helper will write it. Then you can decorate your story by drawing and coloring the different types of bubbles you saw.

"As a class, we're going to write a poem about blowing bubbles. See if you can think of some comparisons about bubbles to put in the poem."

(See lines four, five, and six of the sample poem.) If necessary, give the class hints or first words for each line to keep the ideas flowing.

Example of a free verse poem about bubbles:

> Bubbles float everywhere
> in the air, in the sky
> in my house!
> Some bubbles are as big
> as a beach ball.
> Others are tiny as a bug.
> Bubbles are all the colors
> of the rainbow.
> Blowing bubbles makes me smile.

10. Camera, Lights, Action! (Homework Helper Activity)

Description: Develop the child's appreciation and understanding of reading by helping him or her become an active participant in the reading/listening process in a stage show.

Target Skills: Reading and listening skills

Things You'll Need: Nursery rhymes, poems from children's books or adult poetry anthologies; children's picture books with a simple text and rich illustrations; and props such as toy farm animals to use with nursery rhymes, songs, and poems

Game Plan

1. Act out a nursery rhyme, song, or favorite poem for the children by using motions, sounds, gestures, dance, and different voices for different characters. Encourage them to take turns making their own motions, sounds, and gestures as you tell the story.

2. Once the children have acted out nursery rhymes and short poems, you can progress to longer poems and children's books with simple texts. Act out the story for the class, and as you read, they can take turns acting out the story by using pantomime with puppets or stuffed animals.

3. You can also act out rhymes "on location." For example, if you're at the park, you may want to recite a children's rhyme such as "How Would You Like to Go Up in a Swing?" or "See, Saw, Margery Daw" while the children play on the swing or ride the seesaw.

4. As a follow-up, have the children pretend they're on a stage and are going to be in a show in which they act out nursery rhymes, songs, or poems. You and the children can sing a rhyme such as "Old McDonald Had a Farm," and they can take turns acting it out on a pretend stage with toy farm animals. They can make animal sounds when the song calls for it.

5. As a follow-up, children can put on a similar play with family members. Homework helpers can also recite and act out short adult poems such as e. e. cummings's "hist whist" or children's poems. Then helpers can ask the children to act out the poems with them.

Sample Script: "Today we're going to read some nursery rhymes, sing songs, or read poems and act out the words. Later, you'll put on your own show with one or more other children. I'm going to sing the song, and you can tell me what kinds of things we'll need to put on the show. What kinds of toys will make the show more interesting to the people who watch it?

"You can bring in toy animals from home to use in the show you put on with friends. You can act out your rhyme, poem, or song with one or more friends in the class. Make sounds or motions when you put on your play to make it more interesting.

"You may want to put on a play for your family like the one we did here. You can ask family members to play one or more parts in your play. You and your homework helper can also act out short poems together."

11. Remember a Story

Description: Read a favorite story and encourage the child to fill in missing words and phrases after answering questions about the story. Sharpen memory skills, build vocabulary, and invite the child to participate in the reading process.

Target Skills: Reading, word pronunciation, memory skills, and vocabulary building

Things You'll Need: Favorite picture books

Game Plan

1. Choose a picture book that the children like, one with a simple plot and basic text. Read the story aloud and show the pictures before and after reading each page.

2. Read the same book on at least two consecutive days. Give the children time to turn pages and think about the book. Show them the picture that corresponds to the dialogue and narration on each page. Make your questions about the pictures correspond to the children's knowledge of colors, numbers, naming objects, etc.

3. After the children become familiar with the book, stop at a crucial word or phrase, one that is important to the story. Ask the children if they can say the missing word. If they don't remember, say the word and try again at another section of the book. Eventually, the children will be able to "read" the book to you in their own words or the words they've remembered from your reading to them.

4. Progress from stopping at words and phrases to sentences. The children do not have to give the exact words; giving words that mean the same thing as the text will suffice. The aim is to have the children participate in reading the book.

Sample Script: "Choose one book from these books (in the library, school, home) you'd like to read. I'll read the book and we'll look at the pictures.

"After we've read the book a couple of times, I'll ask you questions. Here are some examples of the kinds of questions I'll ask: 'How many children are in the picture? What color is the dog?' You can take turns giving the answers, or you can point to the pictures in the book to explain something. For example, if I ask 'What happened after the dog fell in the pond?' you can point to this picture of the dog shaking himself and getting the people at the picnic wet.

"Now that you know the story, I'd like you to fill in the missing words and sentences when I stop reading. You don't have to remember the exact words. You can say words that mean the same thing as the words in the book."

12. Clang, Clang Goes the Train

Description: Listen to everyday sounds and sharpen attention to detail; build creativity and listening skills.

Target Skills: Writing, listening skills, and creativity

Things You'll Need: A list of indoor and outdoor sounds the children hear in school and at home (the children will suggest these first, but have a few ideas ready to give as examples).

Game Plan

1. Call the children's attention to the many sounds they hear inside and outside at home and at school. (Save animal sounds for a later activity.) Ask them to identify each sound and to imitate it. (Sample indoor sounds might include: the whooshing of water through a faucet, the splat of an egg against a frying pan, the clatter of dishes in the kitchen, the slapping sounds of hands clapping in a game, and the pop of a balloon bursting. Outside sounds might include: the whistling of wind, the *clang, clang* of an old train approaching, the scream of a siren,

the shouts of children playing, the *bam bam bam* of hammering, and the *pat, pat* of rain against the pavement.)

2. After the children have identified at least three indoor and outdoor sounds and have imitated them, ask them if they'd like to write a short poem as a class about one of the sounds. The class can give ideas to include in the poem as you write them on the board. Then with your help, they can shape their ideas into a poem.

3. As they tell you the words of the poem, write them on the board. Encourage them to use repetition of sounds that remind them of the sounds they're describing. Copy the poem on a poster and ask student volunteers to illustrate it before displaying it.

Sample Script: "Today we're going to talk about the sounds we hear inside and outside. Think of some sounds you hear and be ready to tell me a word that sounds like what you've heard." Give examples. Ask: "What kind of sound does the truck make?"

"Now that we've talked about sounds we hear every day, you'll write a poem together about one of the sounds. Try to use words that sound like the sounds you heard." (Have the children give examples.) "Your poem can rhyme, but it doesn't have to. Which sound would you like to write about?"

Sample poem using a sound:

> Clang, clang, woo, woo.
> I hear the train coming.
> It's rolling down the
> rusty tracks.
> Clang, clang, woo, woo.
> I like to ride the train.
> Do you?

13. Searching for Shapes

Description: Help the child search for shapes and perceive them in common objects. Develop speaking skills and creativity.

Target Skills: Speaking, descriptive ability, and identifying shapes

Things You'll Need: An assortment of objects of different shapes, paper, crayons, colored pencils, blocks, modeling clay, and foods like bread, dough, or cheese for carving shapes

Game Plan

1. Show objects of different shapes and ask the children to name the objects' shapes (square, circle, rectangle, triangle, etc.).

2. Once the children can identify shapes, ask them to think of pictures they can draw using these shapes. (For example, they can draw a snowman with circles and make eyes and noses in triangle shapes, or they can draw a house in the shape of a rectangle.)

3. Have the children draw and color a picture using different shapes. After they have completed their drawings, ask them to exchange them with a partner. Have the partner identify the shapes in the drawing.

4. You can also carve shapes out of modeling clay or foods (bread, cheese, cookie dough). Carve out a face with a food such as sliced cheese. Make nose, eyes, and mouth with different shapes and tack onto the face. The children will enjoy eating the cheese face and the cat made from bread.

5. The children, working with a partner, can create their own shapes using food or clay and a plastic knife.

6. After the children create each shape, ask them to identify the shape and make up a brief story about it for the class.

Sample Script: "We're going to talk about shapes." (Identify the common shapes and ask the children to point to more examples of each shape.) "Everything around us has a different shape. What shape is that lamp? (triangle) Can you find a rectangle in this room? (computer table) Who can spot a circle? (cookie or cracker) You're going to draw a picture using one of the shapes we talked about. Then you'll exchange your picture with a partner and try to figure out what each other drew and tell the object's shape.

"Let's see how we can use shapes to make things with clay or food. How many different things can we make using different shapes? After we make the food shapes, we can eat them.

"You and a partner can make your own shapes with this modeling clay or bread. Then you can make up a short story about the thing you've made with the shape. First name the shape, tell what you made, and then tell the story."

14. Creepy Crawlers and Leaping Lizards (Homework Helper Activity)

Description: Spark interest in reading, writing, and speaking by researching bugs and other creepy creatures to create a picture journal.

Target Skills: Reading, writing (using verbs and adjectives), speaking, and researching, using the Internet and factual books

Things You'll Need: Children's nature books with pictures, children's encyclopedia, storybooks about bugs and other creatures, web access, construction paper, and crayons

Game Plan

1. Gather books that depict and discuss different types of bugs or creatures in which the children express interest. Display the books so that they can look at them to see which creatures intrigue them most. Through a search engine such as Google, find websites about bugs or other creatures that would appeal to the class.

2. Have the children look at pictures of various creatures and ask questions about their characteristics.

3. With the assistance of homework helpers, the children will make a picture journal. Use construction paper and crayons or markers. As a classroom activity, ask the children to draw their favorite creepy creature.

4. Have them draw pictures of what the creature eats and provide a background that shows where it lives. Have them take their drawings home. Ask them to dictate a few sentences about the creature to the homework helper.

5. Have the children bring their drawings along with their sentences about the creature to school. Ask them to show and describe their favorite creepy crawler to the class. Ask them to vote on the creepiest bug and to explain why they chose that one.

6. As a related activity, go on a nature walk and observe live insects. Ask the children to remember the kinds of bugs they see so that they can report on them. Have them consider the bugs' color, size, and actions.

7. Have the children use verbs (action words) to describe for the class how the bugs moved and use adjectives (describing words) to tell about the bugs' appearance. Ask the children which bug they liked best and why.

Sample Script: "We're going to look at bugs and other creatures in these books and on the web, and then you'll draw one in class. You're going to make a picture journal. You'll take your drawing home and think of some sentences to write about the bug you chose. First you'll need to find out a few things about the bug. Your homework helper will help you find more answers on the web. As you say them, your homework helper will write the sentences under your picture.

"Before you draw the bug in class, you'll think about a few questions: How many legs does the bug have? What color is the bug? What does it eat? Where can we find it? Is it okay to touch the bug, or should we stay away from it? After you write sentences with your homework helper, you'll bring your drawing to class and I'll read what you learned about your creepy creature. After the class has heard everyone's report, you'll vote on the creepiest bug.

"Another day we're going to go for a walk and look at some bugs. Remember the kinds of bugs you see so that you can tell the class about them. Remember how the bugs looked and what they did. Was the bug alone or doing something with other bugs like building an ant colony or spinning a web? Did the bug crawl, fly, or move in other ways?"

15. Create a Song (Homework Helper Activity)

Description: Boost writing and speaking skills by having the child create an original song about an important person, place, or thing.

Target Skills: Writing, speaking, and awareness of poetic techniques such as rhythm and use of colorful language

Things You'll Need: Melodies from nursery rhymes or popular songs

Game Plan

1. The children will make up a one- or two-stanza song with a short, simple lyric about someone or something important to them. Bring in simple melodies and have them listen to the melodies to choose the one most appealing to them. They can choose a melody from a popular song, a nursery rhyme, or one from their ethnic heritage.

2. Let the children choose the topic for their songs. It can be a family member or friend, a place they like to visit, or a favorite toy or activity. Play a variety of melodies and let them choose. After choosing the melody in class, have them work with their homework helpers. They will tell the helper why this person, place, or thing is important to them. The helper will take notes on what the child says and will help the child write simple lyrics to go with the melody.

3. The children will bring in their completed songs and will sing them for the class. They will tell the class the stories behind their songs.

Sample Script: "Today we're going to start writing a song about a person, place, or thing that's important to you. I'm going to sing (or play) some music for you. Pick the one you like best and then you and your homework helper will write the words together.

"Once you choose the melody for your song, your helper will take notes on what you say. Then you will make up words to go with the melody of the music you chose.

"After you finish writing your song, you'll bring it to class and play it for us. Then you'll tell us more about the person, place, or thing you wrote about."

Example of song for a place the child likes (sung to the tune of "The Lion Sleeps Tonight"):

> Oh, the seashore, the lovely seashore,
> The magic beach and sand.
> We eat hot dogs and cotton candy
> and go on all the rides.

Example of song for a person (sung to the tune of "London Bridge"):

> I love to go to Grandpop's house,
> Grandpop's house, Grandpop's house,
> I love to play with his big dog
> every summer.
>
> He has swings I like to ride,
> like to ride, like to ride,
> He plays baseball with me too,
> my cool grandpop.

INTERMEDIATE

16. Would You Rather Have an Apple or a Kiwi?

Description: Talk about choices in food, clothing, and other daily routines to give the child practice in speaking and listening skills while helping hone decision-making ability.

Target Skills: Speaking, vocabulary development, thinking skills, and character development (making wise decisions)

Things You'll Need: Base activities upon situations that call for making decisions about choices in daily life, such as what type of clothes to wear and what to eat

Game Plan

1. Everyday situations arise that call for children to make one choice over another. For example, the weather is cloudy, should the child bring an umbrella? The child is hungry, but lunchtime is an hour away. What type of snack would be best? He or she has to choose a book for story time, and all of them look interesting. Which one would be best? Ask the class to think about times they've had to make decisions and to discuss them.

2. Give the children a choice about situations they encounter every day to have them think about how to make a good decision.

3. Whenever children face a simple choice, present them with alternatives and let them decide the best course. If necessary, ask guiding questions to help with the decision-making process.

4. After they make a decision, ask them why they think they've made the best choice.

Sample Script: "Every day you have to make choices. Here's one you can think about now: It looks like it might rain. Do you think it's a good idea to bring an umbrella or should we wait and see what happens?

"It's between snack and lunchtime, and you are getting hungry. We're going to have lunch soon. Which would be better to eat, apple slices or corn chips?" (If most of the children choose corn chips, you can ask why apple slices might be a better option.) Suggested answer: They won't make us full before lunch, and they're better for us.

"Can you think of other times you might have to decide between doing one thing and another?"

17. Sashay, Swing Your Partner (Homework Helper Activity)

Description: Use different types of music to help the child develop critical thinking and speaking skills.

Target Skills: Speaking, listening, writing, and critical thinking

Things You'll Need: CD player and different types of CDs

Game Plan

1. Play a variety of music: popular, country, classical, or children's. Ask the children how the different types of music make them feel (happy, peppy, silly, relaxed, sad, etc.). What does the music remind them of?

2. Have children work with a partner to make up dances to go with one of the pieces of music. They will showcase the dances they made up for the class.

3. Ask the partners to draw a picture using colors that show how the music makes them feel.

4. Ask the children to dictate to the homework helper a one-paragraph story about the music and dance they made up.

5. Read a few stories to the class, or have volunteers tell the stories in their own words.

Sample Script: "I'm going to play different types of music. Tell how the music makes you feel. You and a partner can choose the music you like best. Together you will make up a dance that goes with the music.

"After you practice, you can show the class your dance. How did the music make you feel? Can you name something the music reminds you of? You and your partner can draw a picture using colors that answer these questions about the music and the dance.

"Your homework helper will help you write a story about the dance you made up. Think of a name for your dance. That will be the name of the story. Think about these questions: What was the name of the music? Was the music slow or fast? How did the music make you feel? If you could have a costume for your dance, what would it look like? What colors would your costume be? After you make up your story about the dance, I'll ask some of you to tell the class about it in your own words or, if you want, I will read what you and your helper wrote."

18. What Is It?

Description: Increase sensory awareness in a game that promotes discussion and writing skills.

Target Skills: Speaking, writing, description, and use of sensory imagery in writing

Things You'll Need: Objects found in the classroom or home such as flowers, fall leaves, modeling clay, ice, fruit, and soap

Game Plan

1. Set out a number of objects on a table. Choose things that the children can identify using touch and smell. Assign each object a number.

2. Ask the children to hide their eyes and have them take turns touching and holding one of the objects, which you will hand them. Ask them to describe what they feel and smell. Make a chart on which you write brief notes about each child's observations.

3. After they've tried to identify the objects, show the children the objects. Ask which feeling or scent clues helped them name the objects.

4. Ask the children to draw and color a picture of one of the objects they've looked at.

5. Have the children describe the object to the group, and see if the other students can guess the object from the description.

Sample Script: "When authors write stories, they use touch, smell, and taste to describe what they see. Then we can see the story more clearly. You're going to touch and smell an object and guess what it is from the clues you get. You'll tell me what you feel and smell when you examine the object, and I'll write what you say. Then you'll tell which clues helped you guess the object.

"I'd like you to draw and color a picture of your object and to describe it to the class without saying what it is. See who can name the object you're describing."

19. Hop, Skip, and Jump Letters

Description: Practice the alphabet with the child by saying it to the beat of hopping, skipping, jumping, or jumping rope. The child will progress to naming a noun that begins with each of the letters.

Target Skills: Speaking, learning the alphabet, vocabulary, thinking skills, and following directions

Things You'll Need: Jump rope

Game Plan

1. After you feel confident that the children know the alphabet, have them take turns hopping, skipping, or jumping each letter while saying it aloud. (The children who can jump rope will jump rope to the beat of each letter.)

2. Next, try naming any letter and ask the children to take turns hopping, skipping, or jumping the letters from that point on until you call on the next child.

3. After the children have mastered letters, ask them for examples of (or give examples of) words that begin with each of the letters. Have them take turns hopping, skipping, or jumping the letters with words that begin with the letters (for example, *a, ant*; *b, book*; *c, cow*).

4. You can vary the activity by having the children take turns practicing letters and words in threes. Ask students to stop at a point that you choose and have other students continue.

Sample Script: "We're going to practice letters of the alphabet by hopping, skipping, and jumping as we say the letters. Then I'm going to name a letter, and you'll hop, skip, and jump the next few letters of the alphabet, starting from where I left off.

"Next, you'll take turns practicing letters *and* words. When I say 'Stop,' the next person in line will start hopping, skipping, or jumping letters and words.

"After you take turns practicing letters and words, you'll practice saying letters and words in threes: *a, ape*; *b, bake*; *c, cake*. (If you want, rhyme the words to make them easier to remember.) Each person will take a turn, giving three letters and three words in order."

20. Talking Animals

Description: Practice storytelling and playwriting skills using themes such as courtesy, friendship, and sharing by sculpting animals from modeling clay.

Target Skills: Reading, writing, and character development (polite behavior)

Things You'll Need: Modeling clay in many colors, shoebox, play furniture, books and magazines about animals, and websites featuring animals

Game Plan

1. The children can work with a partner. Help the children research different types of animals in the zoo or in books, magazines, or websites. Ask them to choose an animal to sculpt with clay.

2. After the children learn information about the animals, have them tell about the animals in their own words.

3. The children will model the animal of their choice after those they've seen in the sources you've provided.

4. Help the children sculpt the animals and prepare a shoebox or toy playhouse that will serve as a theater to stage a play with the animals. The play will deal with one main idea related to courtesy, friendship, or sharing. The children can let the animals talk as they would talk to each other.

5. Have the children practice the play with a partner or group and then perform it for an audience.

Sample Script: "We're going to make a playhouse and put on a play with animals you'll make out of clay. First, we'll learn about the animals and how they look and act by going to the zoo, reading about them, or looking on the Internet. I'd like you to think about these ideas when making up your play: courtesy, friendship, and sharing.

"In a play about courtesy, the animals might talk about helping another animal clean up after a game or say how much an animal enjoyed the dinner friends made. In a play about friendship, the animals might welcome a new animal to their playgroup or talk to an older animal that looks lonely. In a play about sharing, the animals might take turns playing with a new toy.

"When you put on your play, you and your partner will make the animals characters in the play. You will pretend you are the voices of the animals. We're going to make a stage out of this shoebox (or chair and sheet). We'll draw a door and use play furniture from a toy house so that the animals can move around and talk to one another. You're going to perform the play for the class after you practice it."

21. Find the Square, Purple Truck

Description: Help the child name common objects in the school or home and identify colors, signs, and shapes while improving speaking skills.

Target Skills: Speaking, listening, descriptive skills, and knowledge of colors, sizes, and shapes

Things You'll Need: Objects of different sizes, shapes, and colors and art materials for home project

Game Plan

1. Display objects of varying sizes, shapes, and colors. You can start with the primary colors and build up to more exotic colors like turquoise and magenta. (Look at crayon colors for ideas.) Discuss size (extra small, small, medium, large, extra large) and shapes (square, rectangle, circle, square, oval).

2. Ask the children to find objects of different sizes, shapes, or colors in the room when you name the characteristics of the object. Focus on a different category or a combination of categories (size, shape, and color) every time you ask the children to give you an object they find.

3. Make it a contest if you want. See who can find the most objects of a given color and/or shape or size in a given amount of time (five minutes or more).

4. After the children (working alone or with a partner) collect all the objects, have them name the objects and give the size, shape, and color of the objects.

Sample Script: "We're going to play a game where I'll ask you to look for things in this room that have a certain size, shape, or color." (Start out by using only one characteristic such as color, and then progress to two or three, such as color and shape.) "Here's an example: 'I'd like you to look for a large toy that is shaped in a circle and has the color red (ball). Next, please find me something small that is shaped like a square and has the color yellow (block).'

"After you've gathered all the objects, I'd like you to take turns naming the objects and to tell me the size, shape, and color of the objects."

22. Tickle My Funny Bone (Homework Helper Activity)

Description: Enhance the child's oral communication skills and problem-solving skills by staging a "dialogue" with stuffed animals.

Target Skills: Speaking, vocabulary building, creativity, and problem solving

Things You'll Need: Stuffed animal of the child's choice

Game Plan

1. Ask the children to choose a stuffed animal so that they and the stuffed animal can engage in a humorous dialogue with another person.

2. Begin by playing the role of the stuffed animal. Read the children a story or sing them a song. Make the stuffed animal tickle or distract you when you're reading or singing.

3. Have the children (one or two volunteers) talk to the stuffed animal and try to persuade it to let you continue the story or song.

4. When problems come up during the day, you can use a stuffed animal to act out problems that arise with individual children. If a child won't eat, you can be the stuffed bear who won't eat. Ask what the child can do to get the bear to eat. Remind the

children to keep a lighthearted approach as they did when the bear tickled you.

5. You can also use the stuffed animal to deal with issues such as being unkind to others, cooperation, or sharing. Ask what the children would say to help the animal deal with the problem. (Set down ground rules: no raising voices or unkind words.)

6. Children and homework helpers can work with the stuffed animal on an ongoing basis to discuss problems that come up at home. The children can come up with solutions with the help of the stuffed animals.

Sample Script: "We're going to pretend this stuffed animal is tickling or teasing me as I read a story. As the animal plays tricks, think of words to say that will convince the animal to stop bothering me.

"We can also act out problems that come up using stuffed animals. For example, I'll pretend I'm the bear and I don't want to take a nap. What can you say to the bear to get him to cooperate? Suppose the bear doesn't want another child to play a game. What can you say to the bear to convince her to let another child play too? When you talk to the bear, keep it light and easy. Why do you think that works better than screaming or using mean words?

"Now you and your homework helper can play the same game with the stuffed animal at home. Sometimes talking with the stuffed animal will help you think of answers if a problem comes up."

23. Cooperative Drawing (Homework Helper Activity)

Description: Help the child identify elements that make up a drawing while fostering vocabulary development and storytelling skills.

Target Skills: Speaking, vocabulary development, storytelling skills, and giving directions

Things You'll Need: A drawing pad; large crayons, colored pencils, or markers; scissors; glue stick; and old magazines

Game Plan

1. The children take turns directing you in drawing a picture. They will figure out all the parts of the whole drawing (the different parts of a face, a house, or a toy) and explain what goes where in the drawing.

2. Encourage the children to aim for more detail in their drawings. Ask them to think of facial expressions they've seen in people they know.

3. The children name each part of the drawing as they add it. Label the different parts of the drawing as they name them (nose, ears, caboose, whistle, etc.).

4. After the children complete the drawings, they will take them home and dictate a brief story about them to their homework helpers.

5. The children will bring their drawings and stories to class. You can read the stories they dictated or they can tell them in their own words.

6. As a related activity, have the children cut and paste pictures from magazines (faces, houses, toys, and desserts, for example). Ask the children to take turns naming the different parts that make up the picture. Label them on the poster as the child identifies them. Have the children tell the story the picture shows.

Sample Script: "You're going to tell me what to put into this drawing to make an interesting picture. What kinds of things would you tell me to draw on a face?" (Suggested answers: eyes, nose, mouth, ears, and hair.) "What else might someone draw on a face?" (Suggested answers: eyebrows, eyelashes, glasses, makeup, a mole.) "How can you make a person look happy or sad?" (Suggested answer: Give them a certain expression in their eyes or mouths or add a smile or frown lines.)

"Now that you've drawn a picture, you're going to take your picture home and write a story about it. You'll tell your homework helper your story and the helper will write it on the page with your picture. Then you'll show your picture and tell the class your story.

"Now that we've made our picture stories, we're going to find pictures in these magazines. Every picture you see is made up of many parts, and every picture tells a story. You're going to name the different parts of each picture, and I'll write them on the poster. Then you'll tell a story about the picture.

"Here are some questions to think about when you make up your story. If your picture shows a house, you might ask: Whose house is in the picture? What are the people in the house doing? If you go into the house, what kind of food would you eat? What types of toys would you play with? What type of pet might the people have?"

24. Alphabet Soup (Homework Helper Activity)

Description: Help the child learn letters of the alphabet and words representing them. The child creates a book with words beginning with different letters of the alphabet.

Target Skills: Letter recognition, vocabulary, speaking, writing, knowledge of adjectives (describing words), and reading

Things You'll Need: Objects and pictures that begin with all the letters of the alphabet; art materials such as construction paper, markers, magazines, and glue stick

Game Plan

1. In class, review the letters of the alphabet and have the children give examples of words beginning with each letter. Whenever you can, display an object that begins with the letter. Go over at least three letters each day. The next day review letters and representative words from the previous day.

2. With the help of the homework helper, the children will make up a booklet with a cover and thirteen pages (one page for two

letters of the alphabet). If they can't find a picture for certain letters, they can draw the object.

3. With the homework helper's assistance, the children will cut pictures from magazines to represent words beginning with each letter of the alphabet. The child will say the word and the helper will write the word beneath the picture.

4. The helpers will have the children dictate or write two or more adjectives (describing words) beneath the name of the object.

5. The children will bring the completed booklets to class with a construction paper cover. Ask them to design covers in class for their alphabet books.

6. Practice the alphabet with the class. Go around the table until all students have taken a turn naming letters of the alphabet in order. Then have students brainstorm words beginning with each letter. Write them on the board as the children say them. See how many words the group can come up with for each letter.

Sample Script: "We're going to practice letters of the alphabet and think of words that begin with each letter. After you can say all the letters, you'll make an alphabet book with your homework helper. Look for pictures in magazines that begin with each letter. If you can't find a picture, draw a picture that begins with that letter.

"You'll also think of at least two describing words which tell about the pictures you find. Here are two examples: *a, antlers*: describing words—*tall, brown*; *b, balloon*: describing words—*big, round, red*. You'll tell your helper the describing words, and the helper will write them on the page with each letter of the alphabet and the pictures you found. Bring your books to class with a cover. We'll decorate the covers in class.

"We're going to practice the alphabet and words that go with each letter. We're going to say the letters of the alphabet in order. Each person will give one letter. When it's your turn, say the next letter of the alphabet. You'll also try to think of as many words as you can that begin with each letter. I'll write them as you say them. Then we'll count how many words you think of for each letter, and I'll write the number after each one."

25. Research a Pet Poster

Description: Teach the child speaking and writing skills while researching information about a household pet.

Target Skills: Reading, speaking, and writing (composing simple sentences), and research skills

Things You'll Need: Library and web resources about the pet you're researching, poster board, markers, and crayons

Game Plan

1. Ask the children which animals they'd like to learn about so that they can create a pet poster. Focus on a specific breed of animal or bird that people have as pets. Learn about the animal from children's nonfiction books about animals, children's reference books, and the Internet. (Some children may want to choose the same pet; they can include different facts about the pet.)

2. To help the children learn about the pets, ask the children specific questions about the pets they're researching.

3. The children will draw and color a picture of the pet they chose. They will dictate two or three simple sentences about the pet, which you will write below the picture.

4. Each child will show the poster to the group and will talk about the pet he or she chose.

Sample Script: "We're going to learn more about a pet, the kind of pet you have at home or one you'd like to have. Before we learn about the pet, we're going to think about some questions. Here are some ideas: What type of animal is the pet? Is the pet big or little? Why does the animal make a good pet? What does the pet eat? What do you have to do to take care of the pet? Why is this pet special? You may want to think of other questions to ask.

"After you learn about the pet, you can draw a picture of it. You'll tell me a couple of things about the pet and we'll write it on the poster with the picture. Then you'll tell the class what you learned about the pet and show them the picture of the pet."

26. Act Out a Song (Homework Helper Activity)

Description: Build speaking skills by having the child act out a song and discuss the process afterwards. Show dramatic expression through gestures.

Target Skills: Speaking, listening, and understanding story elements

Things You'll Need: Songs that appeal to children and CD player

Game Plan

1. Discuss how every song tells a story. Ask the children to think of a song they like and to tell what the song is about.

2. Sing or play a song for the children, and ask them to sing along with you.

3. When you play the song again, act it out with motions and gestures as you sing. Ask the children to act it out in their own way with you.

4. After the children act out the lyrics to display the meaning and emotion of the song, ask them to choose their own song to act out. They can practice with their homework helpers before presenting their songs to the class. They can either play a recording of their song or sing it from memory.

Sample Script: "Have you ever thought how every song tells a story? The song's words are a mini story set to music. I'm going to play a couple of songs. See if you can tell me the story in the song. These questions will help you tell about the story: Who or what is the story about? What happened in the song story? What did you like about the story? Do the words go with the music? If not, what kind of music would you choose for the words?

"Today I'm going to play a song and act it out. You can act it out too. You can use your hands or your body to make the song come to life. You can run, jump, or do whatever you want to act out the song. After we act out a song, you can act out your own song. When you go home, choose a song you like and practice with your homework helper. Then everyone will act out their songs for the class."

27. Once upon a Book

Description: Encourage discussion and promote critical thinking skills with focus questions about the characters and setting of a book.

Target Skills: Reading, speaking, listening, critical thinking skills, and understanding the characters and setting in a story

Things You'll Need: Picture books or longer picture storybooks

Game Plan

1. The children choose books they like from home, school, or the library. Before reading the story, discuss what we mean by characters (people in the story) and setting (where the story takes place).

2. After you read one of the books, go back to selected pages and ask questions to help the children understand characters and setting and the part they play in a story.

Sample Script: "After we read some of the stories you've picked out, we'll go back and talk about some things that the author thinks about when writing a story: characters and setting. The characters are the people in the story. Stories have a main character and other characters that talk and do things in the story to make the story interesting.

"The setting tells where the story takes place. The story could take place in the city, on a farm, or in a faraway land. It could even take place in a spaceship.

"I'll ask you some questions to help you talk about the character and setting of the story." (General questions: Who is the story about? Who is the main person in the story? What are the other characters' names? Where does the story take place? Specific questions: What happened to _____ on this page? What does _____ do about her problem? What happens to _____ at the end of the story?)

28. Make a Weather Book (Homework Helper Activity)

Description: Expand reading, writing, and speaking abilities by having the child make a booklet about different types of weather and about activities to enjoy on different types of days.

Target Skills: Reading, writing, and speaking

Things You'll Need: Construction paper, drawing paper, crayons or markers, children's encyclopedia, children's books about the weather, and children's Internet sites about the weather

Game Plan

1. Talk about the different types of weather prevalent in your part of the country. If the children have never experienced certain kinds of weather such as snow, read to them from a children's encyclopedia, a book about the weather, or the Internet. Learn which types of weather occur in different areas of the country.

2. Talk about activities you can enjoy in different types of weather (sunny, snowy, rainy, and cloudy). Ask, "What would it be like to live in a different part of the country that has different weather conditions than we do? What kinds of things could you do that you couldn't do here?"

3. Help the children make a weather booklet representing the different weather conditions they experience. They will draw a picture of themselves doing something in the different types of weather.

4. The children will take their pictures home and will dictate one or two sentences that describe what they and their friends do to enjoy the weather where they live. The homework helper will write the sentences that describe what the child and friends do to enjoy the day in the different types of weather.

5. The children will bring in their weather booklets and explain their pictures to the class.

Sample Script: "Let's think about what the weather is like where we live. Does the sun shine a lot? Does it ever snow? Do we see a lot or a little rain? Do we ever have hurricanes or tornadoes?

"Here are some questions to think about when we talk about the weather: What are some ways you can have fun in any type of weather? Who can tell me what you can do on a sunny day?" (go to the beach, ride on a swing, or go to the park) "What can you do on a rainy day?" (play indoors with toys or read books) "What can you do on a cloudy day?" (play baseball or tag) "What can you do on a snowy day?" (build a snow fort or igloo, or make snow angels)

"I'd also like you to think about different types of weather in other parts of the country, places that don't have the same kind of weather we do. What would it be like never to have snow or cold weather? How would it feel to have cold weather all the time? Suppose there was a short summer or no summer at all?

"What kinds of things would you do if you lived in a place where the weather was different from the weather you know? What type of weather do you like best? What do you like to do in your favorite kind of weather?

"We're going to make a weather booklet showing how you can have fun in any type of weather. You'll draw the pictures in class about things you can do in different types of weather. Then you'll tell your homework helpers a couple of sentences explaining each of the pictures you drew.

They will write them near the pictures. You'll bring in your weather booklet and tell the class about it."

29. Art Tells a Story

Description: Develop speaking and sentence composing skills while giving the child an appreciation of fine art.

Target Skills: Speaking, writing, appreciation of fine art, and critical thinking skills

Things You'll Need: Fine art books found in the adult section of the library and paints or crayons

Game Plan

1. Gather a variety of art books and tell the children they'll view famous paintings from one or more artists. As the children view the paintings, ask questions to help them learn about the paintings. (You can start out with basic questions and progress to more advanced questions as you examine more works of art.)

2. In response to your questions, have the children give answers in simple sentences about the content of each painting.

3. Ask the children to choose favorite colors from each painting and to paint or color a picture using the colors they see in the painting. The children will explain their paintings to the class. Display the pictures for visitors.

Sample Script: "We're going to look at famous paintings in these books. Each painting tells a story. What do you think it is?" General questions may include: Is the lady in the painting happy or sad? How do you know? (Because she's smiling); What is the horse doing in the barn? (Resting and eating); Why is the man rocking the baby? (So she'll sleep or stop crying).

More open-ended questions for children with advanced speaking skills might include: What is happening in this painting? Why do you think the artist used bright/dark colors in this painting?

"I'd like you to paint or draw and color a picture using your favorite colors from the painting. You'll tell the class about your pictures and the stories they tell. Then we'll hang your pictures on the wall so that everyone who comes here can look at them."

30. Little People Players

Description: Work on speaking and decision-making skills by placing toy people in different situations that deal with topics such as sharing, daily routines, mealtime manners, and getting along with others.

Target Skills: Writing, speaking, character education (courtesy, sharing, getting along with others), and critical thinking skills

Things You'll Need: Toy people figures and pen and paper

Game Plan

1. Give examples of situations that come up in school or at home relating to courtesy, sharing, and getting along with others. Ask the children what they would say and do in a given situation.

2. Tell the children they're going to work in small groups to put on a play about the things they've discussed using the toy people figures. The plays will deal with one main idea.

3. After discussing the above topics, ask the class to brainstorm ideas for short skits about the different topics. Take notes at the board and have the children work on their skits using the ideas they've discussed.

4. The children, along with partners, stage the play, ad-libbing the story line they've decided on. Audience members will discuss the play and ask questions about it.

Sample Script: "We're going to put on a play with toy people figures. First we'll talk about some of the things that happen sometimes in school or at home. We're going to think about courtesy, sharing, and getting along with others.

"I'd like you to think about what you'd say if someone wanted to play with your computer game and you were playing an interesting game." (Possible answer: You can take a turn in a little while.) "Suppose someone ignored you or told you they didn't want to play with you?" (Possible answer: That's okay. I'll play with my other friends now.)

"You and your group can tell me your ideas and I'll write notes about what you say. If you need help when you write your play, the notes will help you think of ideas. You'll practice and put on the play for an audience. The class may want to talk about your play and ask questions about what you wrote."

ADVANCED

31. How Many Things Can a Shoe Box Be?

Description: Nourish the child's verbal powers and creativity by asking how many things a person can make out of one object.

Target Skills: Speaking and creativity

Things You'll Need: Common objects such as a banana, a shoe box, pots and pans, paper plates, and large crayons

Game Plan

1. Show the children a variety of objects and ask what other things they can make from each object to create a toy. Give examples and have partners brainstorm and dictate a list.

2. The partners demonstrate and explain to an audience how one or more objects can be made into a toy.

3. The class can give more ideas for using the objects to make additional toys.

Sample Script: "Here are some things that we use every day. Can you think of how we can make a toy from these things? You're going to work with a partner to make a toy with each of these things and show how you can play with it.

"Here's an example of how you can change something you see at home or school into something else. Here are two bananas. What do we usually do with bananas?" (Suggested answers: eat them, make banana splits, or put them on cereal.) "Let's pretend they're phones, and we can use them to talk to one another.

"Let's look at this shoe box. What else can we do with it?" (Suggested answers: pretend it's a cash register and play store, make it a stage for a play, or make it a treasure chest and fill it with old jewelry.)

"After you tell what else you can make with the objects on the table, we'll ask the class what kinds of toys they would make from the same objects."

32. Rip-It, Meow, and Wolf Wolf (Homework Helper Activity)

Description: Sharpen the child's auditory sense by identifying outside and inside sounds; stimulate speaking and writing skills.

Target Skills: Listening, speaking, writing, and sensory awareness (auditory)

Things You'll Need: Outside and inside sounds

Game Plan

1. Take the children outside and listen for different sounds. Ask what each sound represents. Point out that some sounds come from nature (birds calling, dogs barking, and frogs croaking), and others come from people (sirens, car horns honking, and children shouting). Inside we hear different kinds of sounds like chairs scraping, people walking, chalk against a chalkboard, pots and pans rattling, and water running.

2. The children take turns naming the sounds and imitate each one. The children also imitate the sounds they heard for another child to see if he or she can identify the sound. Point out that sometimes people hear things differently.

3. After the children have listened to different sounds for a couple of days, ask them to dictate a mini story (about two or three sentences) to their homework helper about the sounds they

heard. The children will bring in the story, and you can read it to the group (or the child can retell it).

Sample Script: "Today when we go outside, we'll listen for sounds. Pick one sound, tell what kind of sound it was, and imitate the sound. Did a person or animal make the sound? Is it a serious sound (an ambulance siren), a funny sound (a frog croaking), a happy sound (a person laughing), or an excited sound (a dog barking because it wants to play)?

"Now I'd like you to think about what kinds of sounds you hear inside." (Suggested answers: a teapot whistling, a dryer tumbling, music playing, or a cat purring.)

"You'll tell your homework helper a mini story about one sound you heard outside or inside, and your helper will write it down. You'll bring in your story to share with the class."

𝟹𝟹. If I Were Yellow, I'd Be a Banana

Description: Fine-tune the child's visual sense and ability to describe colors and objects.

Target Skills: Writing, speaking, and sensory awareness (sight)

Things You'll Need: Small crayon boxes with basic colors and large boxes of crayons with many colors

Game Plan

1. Have enough small and large boxes of crayons to share with the class. Tell the children they're going to look at different colors and match the colors with objects they've seen.

2. Look at colors in the small crayon box with the basic colors, and ask the children to take turns choosing a color. Ask them to name the color and to think of an object that they've seen of that color.

3. Ask the children to take turns saying a sentence using the words, "If I were (name a color), I'd be a/an (name an object)."

Give examples for them to model. You can use any category you want for the objects such as fruits, toys, something in nature, or you can mix categories to simplify the activity.

4. To make the activity more challenging, offer the children more exotic colors from the large crayon box and ask them to work with partners to complete a sentence using an object that might be that color. Tell them the name of the color and ask them to repeat it. Then have them say the sentence, listing an object they think would fit the color.

Sample Script: "You're going to take turns choosing a crayon and think of something that matches the color you chose. Then you're going to say sentences like the ones I give you. Compare the color with something that's the same color. Here are some examples of sentences using fruits: If I were yellow, I'd be a banana; If I were purple, I'd be a grape; If I were red, I'd be a strawberry. In these sentences, I used the words 'If I were _____, I'd be _____.' Use these same words when you think of your own sentences.

"Then you're going to think of other things besides fruits that are the same colors as the crayons: for example, toys or something in nature.

"Now that we've done basic colors, let's look at more colors in this large box of crayons. This time you'll work with a partner. This color is a pinkish purple. It's called magenta. Can you and your partner make up a sentence about it using the same words you used with the other colors? Here's an example: If I were magenta, I'd be a sunset. Here's another one with a special shade of green: If I were lime green, I'd be a lollipop. Now let's see what you come up with." (Award small prizes like stickers for the most original sentences.)

34. Throw Some Words Around

Description: Learn parts of speech and work on vocabulary skills by playing a ball game.

Target Skills: Speaking, listening, parts of speech, and vocabulary

Things You'll Need: A lightweight ball that bounces

Game Plan

1. Explain that any person, place, or thing is called a noun. After giving examples, ask the children to list nouns in each category: person, *sister*; place, *school*; and thing, *playhouse*.

2. Tell the children that they're going to take turns playing catch with you and learn about nouns at the same time. You'll give a category and they will say a word each time one of you throws the ball to the other. For example, if you say *person*, you'll throw the ball and the child will catch it. The child will state the name of a person such as *cousin*. Then he'll throw the ball back to you. You'll give another category and the child will provide an example. Switch roles every so often, with the child listing the category and you giving the example.

3. After the children practice the game, they can play the game with each other and make it a contest. The child who continuously gives an answer (in a reasonable amount of time) wins. Dropping or missing the ball doesn't count against the players.

Sample Script: "We're going to play a game and learn about nouns. Nouns are persons, places, or things. Who can give an example of a person/place/thing?

"We're going to play a game of catch with nouns. I'll say *person, place,* or *thing*, and you'll give a word that fits it. For example, if I say *person*, you could say *singer*; if I say *place*, you could say *seashore*; if I say *thing*, you could say *merry-go-round*.

"Every time I say a word and you give an answer, we'll throw the ball to each other. Don't worry if you miss the ball. Just pick it up and try again. Later, you'll take a turn saying the type of word, and I'll name a person, place, or thing that fits. You'll also play the game with another child and we can make it a contest."

35. Funny, Funnier, Funniest

Description: Teach how to use adjectives and how to compare them by using toys and pictures as props.

Target Skills: Comparison of adjectives, speaking, and listening

Things You'll Need: Musical instrument or CD player, stuffed animals of varying degrees of softness, three toys of progressively larger sizes, and three silly jokes, such as knock-knock jokes

Game Plan

1. Play a musical instrument or music at three different pitches. As you play it, stop after each note and label it *loud*, *louder*, *loudest*. Then play music that is *soft*, *softer*, and *softest*.

2. Gather stuffed animals of varying degrees of softness or sizes. Ask the children to identify them as *soft*, *softer*, *softest* or *big*, *bigger*, *biggest*.

3. Show other toys or objects of different sizes and arrange them in size order (big to biggest or small to smallest). Ask the children to state the adjective that refers to each size.

4. Next, think of something intangible like jokes. Tell three jokes and ask the children to rank them in order of funny, funnier, and funniest. (When comparing intangibles, children may have different opinions.)

Sample Script: "When we talk about something like music we can compare one sound to another by using describing words. We can say that one sound is loud, the next is louder, and the other is loudest. We can also say that one sound is soft, the next is softer, and the other is softest. I'll play music, and you tell me the describing word I should use to tell about the music.

"Let's touch these stuffed animals and compare them using different describing words. Which is soft, softer, and softest? Which one looks big, bigger, biggest?

"Now we'll look at some other toys. Tell me describing words I can use to compare the sizes of the different toys. What about these blocks (*small*, *smaller*, *smallest*) and these trucks (*big*, *bigger*, *biggest*)?

"For our last activity, I'm going to tell you three jokes. Tell me which joke is funny, which is funnier, and which is the funniest joke. People sometimes have different ideas of what is funny, so you can give different answers and still be right."

36. The Loose Goose Rides the Red Caboose

Description: Encourage the child to have fun rhyming words and composing outrageous sentences.

Target Skills: Speaking, writing, and rhyming

Things You'll Need: A few simple rhymes that you make up and a rhyming dictionary (optional)

Game Plan

1. Have a list of rhyming words ready. Ask the children to think of words that rhyme with the words you've presented. (If they can't think of a rhyming word, give pantomime clues.)

2. Give the children a few words from the rhyming dictionary or your list, and ask them to take turns dictating words that rhyme with the words you give them. Write the words on the board.

3. Have them dictate humorous sentences using the rhymes you gave them and other rhymes they make up.

4. The children will brainstorm rhyming words with a partner. See how many rhyming words they can think of for each word. Ask the partners to make up a sentence for one set of rhyming words and to say their sentence for the group.

Sample Script: "We're going to write some funny sentences using rhyming words. First we'll practice rhyming words. Here are some examples: *bat, hat, sat; sail, tail; see, bee; eat, feet.* Then you'll tell me one or two words that rhyme with these words and other words I give you. I'll write the rhyming words on the board. Then you'll make up a funny sentence using the two or three rhyming words. Here are two examples: The purple *whale* had a tiny *tail;* the *loose goose* rides the red *caboose.*

"Next, you and a partner will think of your own rhyming words. You can make up your own funny sentences with one set of rhyming words. I'll write them down, and then we'll tell the class your sentences."

37. My Favorite Place Poster (Homework Helper Activity)

Description: Build vocabulary and strengthen descriptive ability in composing sentences by creating a poster about a favorite day trip or vacation.

Target Skills: Writing (paragraph development) and speaking

Things You'll Need: Small poster board or heavy paper and markers or crayons

Game Plan

1. The homework helper asks the child to describe a favorite place in three or four sentences. The helper uses the guiding questions in the sample script to shape the paragraph and writes the answers as the child answers them.

2. The homework helper copies the completed paragraph onto the poster board. The helper reads the completed paragraph, and the child thinks of an ending sentence, which the helper adds to the paragraph.

3. When the children bring their paragraphs to class, have them decorate their posters with crayons, markers, and glitter or stickers. Ask them what they want to call their stories and write their titles on the posters.

4. Display the posters and have them share their observations about a favorite place with the class.

Sample Script: "I'd like you to think of a place you visited with your family or friends, a place which you'd like to return to again because you liked it very much. You and your homework helper are going to make up a story about your favorite place.

"You'll tell your helper the story, and the helper will write it on this poster. Then you'll bring the poster back to class and decorate it. You'll tell me what you want to call your story, and then you'll show your favorite place poster to the class and tell them your story in your own words.

"Here are some questions to think about when you describe your favorite place: Where do you go on vacation? Who goes with you? Who do you like best about the place? When do you go there? (winter, summer, fall) Why is this your favorite place? You'll write a story using your answers to these questions. What would you like to call your story?"

38. A Time for Everything (Homework Helper Activity)

Description: Give the child practice in speaking and writing and build organizational skills by making a booklet about daily routines.

Target Skills: Speaking, writing, organizational skills, and understanding the concept of time of day

Things You'll Need: Construction paper, white paper, and crayons or markers

Game Plan

1. Have the children brainstorm lists of things they do during different times of day (morning, afternoon, and night). Write the list on the board as they dictate.

2. After the children have completed the list, ask them to name the one thing they like best about each part of the day. Draw a star next to their favorite activities.

3. Remind the children that a sentence is a complete thought and model sentences for them. Ask them to take turns dictating sentences about the things they like best. Write the sentences on the board, read them, and ask why they are sentences. (They have complete thoughts and they make sense.)

4. The children and homework helpers work together to make a booklet about the three times of day. The helper asks the child to make up a sentence about a favorite activity during the morning, afternoon, and night. The helper writes the child's sentences on unlined paper to make a booklet, allowing one page for each of the three times of day. The helper staples the pages.

5. When the children bring the booklets to class with the completed sentences, have them draw pictures of the activities they wrote about under the sentences. Ask them to draw a cover and make up a title for their time of day booklet.

6. The children can display their booklets at home and ask family members to tell about their favorite times of day.

Sample Script: "We can divide the day into three times: morning, afternoon, and night. What kinds of things do you do in the morning?" (wake up, eat breakfast, play outside, and look at books) "What do you do in the afternoon?" (eat lunch, take a nap, play with friends, and play with my toys) "What do you do at night?" (eat dinner and dessert, read a bedtime story, and go to sleep)

"First you'll tell me a couple of sentences about what you like to do during each part of the day. When you tell me your ideas, please say them in sentences. Sentences are complete thoughts that make sense." (Sample answers: I like the morning because I play outside on the swings; I like the afternoon because we have art and can paint at the easel; and I like the night because I like to read stories with my mom and dad before bedtime.)

"You and your homework helper are going to make a booklet about the three different times of day. You'll think of a sentence about why you like each time of day, and you or your helper will write it. Make a different page for each time of day. When you bring the booklet back to class, you'll draw a picture for each sentence and make a cover.

"After you've finished your booklet, you'll think of a title and I'll write it on the cover. Then you'll show your booklet to your family and ask them to tell you about their favorite time of day."

39. Design a Greeting Card (Homework Helper Activity)

Description: Sharpen sentence-writing skills and creativity by making a greeting card.

Target Skills: Writing (sentence construction), reading, and character development (thoughtfulness)

Things You'll Need: List of sentences to complete, white paper folded in half, markers, crayons, glue stick, glitter or stickers, and free Internet greeting card sites

Game Plan

1. Ask the children to create a greeting card in the form of a short free verse poem for a friend or someone in the family. They can write it for a special occasion or to let the person know they care about them.

2. Write parts of sentences and provide the homework helpers with the partial sentences (listed under "sample sentences" in the Sample Script). The homework helpers will help the children turn the sentences into a greeting card message.

3. The helper will copy the verse onto the white paper and will fold it once into the shape of a card. The child will bring the card to class along with a stamped addressed envelope. Ask the children to illustrate their cards with a drawing, glitter, and stickers. The helper will help the child mail the card.

4. As a follow-up, the homework helper can find an Internet website that provides free greeting card templates. The child will choose one after the helper reads sample verses. The helper will help the child send the card via e-mail.

Sample Script: "You and your homework helper are going to make a greeting card to send to a friend or relative. I'm going to send home these sentences to help you write your card. If you'd like, you can make up your own sentences instead."

Sample sentences:

Dear _____,
You are a good friend because _____. We have fun when we _____.
I hope you _____.
Your friend,

_____

"After you and your homework helper finish writing your card, you'll bring it in and decorate it. Then you and your helper will mail it.

"Another time, your helper can help you look on the Internet and choose a card to send another friend or relative. (The helper can type 'children's greeting cards' into a search engine and find websites that offer cards specifically for children.) The helper will read you some verses, and you can pick the verse and picture you like best. You can send your card to someone."

40. Climb a Family Tree (Homework Helper Activity)

Description: Develop speaking, writing, and organizational abilities by building and describing a family tree.

Target Skills: Speaking, writing, and organizational skills and character development (fosters family closeness)

Things You'll Need: White paper, construction paper for cover, colored markers, snapshot of child, and diagram of a family tree made by the teacher

Game Plan

1. Explain to the children that a family tree contains the names of all different family members a person has. The children will

work with their homework helpers to fill in a family tree. The helper will write the family members' names on the branches of the family tree.

2. Have the children ask the helpers to write down the names of parents, siblings, grandparents, and aunts and uncles in the branches of the family tree. The children will dictate the names of family members as the helpers write them.

3. The helpers will ask the children to tell one interesting fact about each person in the family tree, and the helper will write the sentence near the person's name.

4. The children will bring their completed family trees to class. Have the children place pictures of themselves on the cover. The children can show classmates their family tree booklets and tell them about their families.

Sample Script: "Have you ever heard of a family tree? You're going to make one with your homework helper. I'm going to give you a picture that has a big tree with many branches. You and your helper will fill in the branches with names of your family members. Ask your helper to write down the names of all the people in your family tree as you say their names.

"The words on the tree will help you and your helper know where to write the names of the people in your family. Put your grandparents' names at the top of the tree; your parents' names will go under theirs. You can put your aunts' and uncles' names beside your parents'. You'll write your name and your brothers' and sisters' names under your parents' names.

"Find out one fact about each person in your family tree. You'll say it, and your helper will write it near that person's name.

"In class, you'll make a cover for your family tree booklet and tell the other children about your family tree."

41. Describe Foods in an Adjective Journal (Homework Helper Activity)

Description: Study adjective usage by using the senses to describe familiar foods.

Target Skills: Writing, parts of speech, and using sensory images

Things You'll Need: Prepared food journal sheets (see #3, Game Plan), lined paper, ruler, and adhesive stars

Game Plan

1. Explain to the children that they will keep a food journal using describing words (adjectives).

2. Give examples of describing words as they relate to food (*tasty, hot, salty, colorful, spicy, chewy, crunchy*).

3. Make the food journal ahead of time by drawing three vertical lines on lined paper. Divide the chart into columns and label them *taste*, *sight*, and *touch*. Write the different foods' names on the left side of the chart. Distribute one food journal to each child.

4. At meal or snack time, ask the child to fill in the chart with one describing word (adjective) for each of the three categories. You'll record these three observations in a food journal that you can add to periodically. The children will continue this assignment at home the following week with the homework helper.

5. At the end of the second week, have the children place a star next to their favorite foods in the food journal. They will also draw a picture of the food next to its name.

Sample Script: "After lunch or snack time this week, we're going to work on a food journal. I'm going to make a chart so that you can tell about the different foods we eat. Next week you'll take the chart home. You and your homework helper will keep a food journal for a week.

"For your journal at school and at home, I'd like you to think about the taste of the food (plain, salty, or crunchy), how it looks (color, size, and shape), and how it feels when you eat it (hard, soft, mushy, or creamy). We call these words *describing words* or *adjectives*. Here's an example: apple—**Taste**: sweet; **Looks**: red, round; **How it feels**: crunchy. You'll draw a picture of the food and put a star next to the three foods you ate that you liked best."

42. Fish for Nouns

Description: Teach nouns and describing words (adjectives) and give practice writing sentences by playing a "name the object and describe it" game.

Target Skills: Identifying nouns, writing (sentence construction), speaking, listening, and describing objects

Things You'll Need: A number of objects that you can classify as nouns, a box or laundry basket, and paper and pens

Game Plan

1. Place a variety of common objects in a laundry basket. Explain that a person, place, or thing is called a *noun* and that words that describe nouns are called *describing words* or *adjectives*. The children will name and describe things that you choose from the laundry basket.

2. Ask the children to choose an object from the laundry basket without looking. Have them name and describe the object they choose and tell some things they can do with the object.

3. As they dictate one or two sentences about the objects, write what they say.

Sample Script: "Today we are going to learn about nouns and describing words. Nouns name persons, places, or things. Describing words tell about nouns. I've put some things in this laundry basket. I want you to pretend you're fishing for an object.

"Choose something from the basket without looking, and say what the object is. Tell me one or two sentences that describe the objects and talk about some things you can do with the object. I'll write what you say and read it back to you. Then you can tell me if there's anything else you want to say about it.

"Here are some examples of what you can say about the objects: This is a pack of crayons (I can color pictures with them); This is a red ball (I can play catch or baseball with it); This is a blue wallet (I can put money in the wallet and buy ice cream at the store)."

43. Make a Special Character Poster (Homework Helper Activity)

Description: Practice using descriptive adjectives by making a poster of a favorite book, movie, or cartoon character.

Target Skills: Speaking, writing, listening, and identifying and using adjectives

Things You'll Need: Favorite picture books, paper and pen, medium-sized poster board and markers

Game Plan

1. Find picture books that feature an interesting hero or heroine. Ask the children to look over the books and to vote on the one that most appeals to them.

2. Explain that they are going to make posters about the main character in the book. Ask them what the main character is wearing and about his or her hairstyle.

3. The children dictate a list of describing words (adjectives) that describe the character. Copy the list and send it to the homework helper. The children will use the list to compose a mini story (two to three sentences) about the character.

4. The homework helper will write the child's mini story on the poster. The children will bring their stories to class and draw a picture of the main character to illustrate them. Read mini stories to the class and let the children show their pictures.

Sample Script: "I'd like you to choose one of these picture books. You'll choose your favorite and you'll vote on the book that you want me to read.

"As I read the story, I'd like you to think about the main character in the story. What is he or she like? What words would you use to tell about the character? Tell me from looking at the picture what the character is wearing and what he or she looks like.

"Let's make up a list of words that describe the main character. I'll send them to your homework helper. The helper will help you write a mini story about the character. You'll think about the character and the describing words and then you'll tell your helper the story. The helper will write your story on the poster. Then you'll bring your story to class and draw a picture of the main character. You can show your picture to the class, and I'll read your stories to everyone."

44. Design a Noun Drawing (Homework Helper Activity)

Description: Practice speaking skills and teach attention to detail and planning by having the child direct you in drawing a picture. Also gives practice identifying nouns.

Target Skills: Speaking, giving directions, attention to detail, and identifying nouns

Things You'll Need: Construction paper, markers or colored pencils, and overhead projector or large drawing pad

Game Plan

1. Discuss and give examples of nouns. Let students take turns directing you in drawing pictures of nouns on the board or a large drawing pad. If they need ideas, ask leading questions to help them complete the drawings.

2. After the children complete the pictures, ask them to name what they have drawn and to tell if the drawing is a person, place, or thing. See if they can name other nouns in the picture.

3. The children repeat the procedure with the homework helpers and bring in the completed picture. They take turns showing

their pictures and naming as many nouns as they can in the pictures.

Sample Script: "You're going to take turns helping me draw a picture of a noun or naming word. Then you and your homework helper will draw a picture together. You'll bring in the picture and talk about it to the class.

"A noun is any person, place, or thing. Think of a noun you want me to draw. You can describe it and I'll draw it the way you tell me. Think about your drawing before you tell me and your helper what to put in it.

"Here are some questions to think about: What would the person in this spaceship look like? (small head, one eye) What would we find at the amusement park? (merry-go-round, cotton candy) What should we put on this house? (chimney, windows, a door)

"Now that we've finished our picture, do you see any other nouns in the picture? What other nouns do you see in this picture of a garden?" (Suggested answer: flower, bug.) "How about this snowman?" (pipe, broom)

"Just as you've done with our class drawings, you'll tell your homework helper what you want in your own drawing of a person, place, or thing, and the helper will follow your directions. You'll tell your helper what you've drawn and the names of any other persons, places, or things in your drawing.

"You'll bring your drawings to school and tell the class about all the nouns (persons, places, or things) in your drawings."

PART II
ACTIVITIES
AGES 4-6

BASIC

45. Solve the Riddle

Description: Help the child learn about nouns and using description in a sentence by solving simple riddles. Also practice using complete sentences.

Target Skills: Speaking, writing (description), and parts of speech (nouns) as they relate to writing

Things You'll Need: Simple riddles about commonly found objects in the school or home

Game Plan

1. Tell the children they're going to play "Guess the riddle." The riddle will use descriptions to give clues to answer the riddle with a naming word (noun).

2. Prepare five to ten simple riddles. Use descriptions that relate to the objects you want the children to guess. Use nouns to identify objects.

3. After you describe the object in a simple riddle, the children will take turns giving the answer to the riddle in a complete sentence.

4. After the children have solved your riddles, ask them to make up their own riddles to ask another child. They will describe an object, and the child guessing the riddle will use a complete sentence.

Sample Script: "Today you're going to solve some riddles. A riddle is a word puzzle that asks a question. I'm going to describe something in a riddle, and you will tell me the answer to the riddle in a complete sentence. Start your sentence with the words 'I am a _____' and give the answer to the riddle at the end of the sentence. Let's practice:

> When you sit on my soft seat, I ride you around the block.
> What am I?
> (Answer: I am a bike.)

> I am a red rectangle that holds something to eat.
> What am I?
> (Answer: I am a lunch box.)

> I landed on a flower and someone tried to catch me. I am blue, red, and yellow.
> What am I?
> (Answer: I am a butterfly.)

"Now it's your turn to make up a riddle. You can make up a riddle with a partner and ask the class who knows the answer. Tell about the object you want someone to guess and ask, 'What am I?' Someone will tell you the answer to the riddle in a complete sentence."

46. Tell Me a Story (Homework Helper Activity)

Description: Build ability to tell a story in sequence and practice composing story questions.

Target Skills: Speaking and writing (storytelling in sequence)

Things You'll Need: Pen and paper

Game Plan

1. Talk about the idea of sequence in a story, how one thing happens after another. This time let the children tell *you* a story.

They will work as a group, first planning the events of the story. Each child will take a turn adding ideas to an original story until the story is complete.

2. After they plan the story, have the children build a story around the plot. Write it as they dictate it. Then help them polish the story. Read the edited story back to them.

3. The children can plan their own stories at home with the help of a homework helper. The children will then dictate their stories to their helpers, who will help them revise their stories. The helpers will help the children write questions to ask the other children about their stories.

4. The children will bring in their stories and will read them to the class.

Sample Script: "You're going to write your own story as a class. First, we'll write a story together in class. Then you'll work with your homework helper to plan your own story. You can tell about something that really happened, or you can make up a story. You can also think about a story we've read and make the character in that story have another adventure.

"Now you're ready to write your own story. After you think of what you want to write about and plan your story, you will dictate it to your helper. You'll bring in your story, and I'll read it to the class. Then you can ask the class questions about your story."

47. Grab Bag Gold

Description: Develop imagination and speaking skills by asking the child to think of different games they can play with objects from a homemade grab bag.

Target Skills: Speaking and imaginative skills

Things You'll Need: A few interesting objects from the dollar store, a paper grocery bag, and pen and paper

Game Plan

1. The children will each choose an object from a grab bag. They will close their eyes when they choose the objects. (Objects may include: shiny stickers, costume jewelry, a plastic kazoo or harmonica, a toy car, a magic wand, and plastic containers.)

2. Once they choose an object, they will think of different games they can play with it. Make a chart for each object and the children (or you) will write their ideas for games.

3. Have the children tell the class one idea for how to use their object, and ask the other children for their ideas. Add these ideas to the list. Arrange a playtime when the children can play with the objects in the grab bag.

Sample Script: "Choose something from this grab bag and think of different ways you can play with the object. After you think of how you can play with the object, we'll make a chart. I will write the name of the object at the top of the paper, and you will tell me the ways you can play with it.

"Here are some ideas for how you can play with some of the objects: plastic container (turn it into a toy bank); stickers (decorate a picture you draw); a plastic kazoo or harmonica (put together a band with friends); jewelry (set up a jewelry store); a magic wand (go on a new adventure every time you wave it).

"I'd like you to tell the class how you would play with each object. Then we'll see if anyone else can think of other ideas for playing with the object. We're going to have a special playtime when you can take turns playing with all the objects."

48. Cut and Paste Collage

Description: Increase the child's descriptive abilities and sharpen the kinesthetic sense by creating a collage that tells a story.

Target Skills: Writing, speaking, and decision making

Things You'll Need: Magazines, scissors, glue stick, and construction paper

Game Plan

1. Ask the children to think of a theme for a collage that they'll make with magazine pictures. They can build their collages around school, a favorite activity, favorite foods, friends, play, or a special interest.

2. Ask them to cut out and arrange pictures that show the collage's theme and to arrange them in a way that looks best.

3. After the children paste each picture on the collage, ask them to describe the picture in one or two sentences. Note that a sentence is a complete thought. Give examples of sentences and nonsentences. Have them dictate or write the sentences on the collage.

4. Have the children explain the collage to the class. Ask the class to tell one thing they learned from the collage.

Sample Script: "A collage is a combination of different pictures pasted together on a paper to show one idea. Today you're going to make a collage. You'll cut out pictures from magazines and glue them onto construction paper. Can you think of any ideas for making a collage?" (Suggested answers: pets, sports, healthy foods, toys you like to play with.)

"Once you've decided on an idea, you can cut out your pictures. Think about which picture you want to put in the center. Think about how you want to arrange the other pictures around the main picture and then glue them to the construction paper.

"You'll write or dictate one or two sentences about your collage and place them anywhere you want on the collage. A sentence is a thought, but it's never a part of a thought. Here's a sentence you might use: 'My collage is about pets. The big picture shows pets you might want to have.' If you said, 'Pets you might like,' that would be a part of a sentence, not a complete sentence.

"After you make your collage, you'll show it to the class and explain it. The other children will tell you one thing they learned from your collage."

49. Picture a Story (Homework Helper Activity)

Description: Give the child practice in putting thoughts into words. Help boost imaginative powers by having the child make up a story using a book with few words and many pictures.

Target Skills: Writing (elements of a story) and reading

Things You'll Need: A selection of vivid picture books with few or no words

Game Plan

1. Choose richly illustrated picture books with few or no words. Let the children choose a book to tell their own stories.

2. Tell the children they're going to make up stories using the pictures in a book to help them think of ideas. Give them time to look at all the pages of the book they're going to use to tell the story.

3. The story should have a beginning, which sets the stage for the action; a middle, which fills in the details of the story; and an end, which tells what happens to the main character or how the character changes.

4. Have the children tell the class a story based on the pictures in the book they chose. Encourage the class to ask questions about the story, and have the child who made up the story answer them.

5. Ask the children to picture another story with their homework helpers. Have them bring in the book and tell the class their stories.

Sample Script: "I've brought in some picture books that have very few or no words. You're going to look at all the pages and make up your own story to go with the pictures in the book."

"Every story we read has a beginning, middle, and end, and I'd like to see these three parts in your story too. What do you think you see at the beginning part of every story?" (We learn about who and what the story is about.) "What do you see in the middle of the story?" (We learn more about the people in the story and what the story's about.) "What happens in the end of a story?" (We learn what happens to the main character and how the author wraps things up.)

"After you make up your story, you'll show everyone the pictures in the book and tell the class your story. They may want to ask you questions or talk about your story.

"You and your homework helper will work together to tell another story with a picture book that has few or no words. Then you'll bring in the book, show the pictures, and tell everyone your story."

50. Sometimes Clouds Are More Fun than Sunshine

Description: Boost word power and writing ability by showing how people can see the same thing but perceive it differently while viewing cloud formations.

Target Skills: Writing (description), vocabulary, speaking, and character development (understanding of others' viewpoints)

Things You'll Need: Pen and paper

Game Plan

1. Choose a day when you see a lot of distinctly formed clouds in the sky. Ask the children (working with partners) to look at cloud formations and to think about what they see in them. Ask them to draw a picture of what they see and to describe it.

2. Compare the partners' different observations about what they saw in the same cloud.

3. Have partners write or dictate a description of what they saw in one or more clouds they observed.

4. Ask them to share their pictures and descriptions of the cloud formations with their classmates.

Sample Script: "You're going to look at clouds with a partner to see what kinds of pictures you see in them. Then you're going to compare what you saw with what your partner saw.

"People often see different things when they look at clouds. You might see a lion, your friend might see a dragon, and I might see a golden retriever. Why do you think that is?" (Possible answer: People are not the same and they see things differently.) "There is no right or wrong answer when looking for cloud pictures. If you can explain why you saw something, that's a good enough explanation.

"Can you think of any other times that people might see different things while looking at the same thing?" (Possible answer: in a painting, in a design, or an optical illusion.)

"After you and your partner say what you saw in the clouds, both of you will draw a picture of what you saw. After you're finished with your drawing and description, you'll tell everyone what you saw. Your partner will tell what he or she saw too. You'll both pass around your pictures and explain what you saw to the class."

51. Flowers Brighten Our World

Description: Expand descriptive skills by compiling a booklet of flower pictures.

Target Skills: Reading, writing, and speaking

Things You'll Need: Magazines containing pictures of flowers, white paper and construction paper, markers, pen, scissors, and glue stick

Game Plan

1. Talk about how flowers differ in color, size, and scent and how some come up every year and others need to be planted annually.

2. Tell the children they're going to make a flower booklet (three to six pages). Ask them to cut out pictures of flowers

that they like and glue them to the pages (one flower to a page). They'll write the name of the flower on the page and write (or dictate) a sentence or two describing the colors of the flowers. They will also describe the size and shape of the flowers and the scent, if they can identify it. On the last page, they will write the name of their favorite flower and tell why they chose it.

3. After they complete their booklets, they will show them to the class. They will read or tell the class their stories about the flowers.

4. The children will decorate the covers of their booklets and give them to a family member as a gift.

Sample Script: "I've brought in some flowers (or pictures of them) to show you that there are many different types of flowers. Some are big, some are little, some have a strong scent, and some have no scent at all. Some flowers like zinnias come up every year, but some like geraniums need to be planted every year. Do you have any flowers in your garden? Tell me their names and describe how they look.

"I'd like you to cut out some pictures of flowers from these magazines and glue one flower to each page. Write what type of flower it is and write or dictate your description of the flowers.

"On the last page of your booklet, write (or dictate) a sentence or two telling which is your favorite flower and explain why. You'll give your book to someone in your family."

52. Opposites Are Everywhere (Homework Helper Activity)

Description: Look for opposites in everyday surroundings. Give examples of opposites and write sentences using them.

Target Skills: Writing, speaking, and listening

Things You'll Need: Small notepad to use as a journal, highlighter, and pen

Game Plan

1. Explain the concept of opposites and give examples. Ask the children (with the assistance of their homework helpers) to keep an opposites journal for a week, observing opposites in their everyday lives.

2. The children will write or dictate at least ten examples of opposites to their homework helpers in their journals. They will then choose five pairs of opposites for which they'll write or dictate a sentence, highlighting the opposites in each sentence.

3. After they complete their opposites journals, ask the children to share their opposites with the class and to give sentences for one another's examples.

4. Give small prizes for the funniest and the most unusual opposites (words or sentences).

Sample Script: "What do we call these pairs of words: *hot, cold; small, big; full, empty; sad, happy; silly, serious?*" Ask a volunteer to explain what we mean by opposites (when things are different from each another).

"I'd like you to keep an opposites journal for a week and then we'll come back and talk about the examples you wrote. Write (or dictate) at least ten of them to your homework helper. I'd like you to choose five pairs of opposites and to write a sentence using both words in the sentence. Highlight the opposites in each sentence.

"After you've finished your opposites project, we'll come back and talk about your examples. You'll also tell everyone your examples and give the class a chance to give their own sentences for a few of them. I'll give a prize for the funniest and the most unusual opposites."

53. Bubble Up a Poem (Homework Helper Activity)

Description: Jump-start creative writing ability by using a bubble diagram (similar to a cluster diagram) to spark an idea for writing a class poem.

Note: To learn more about clustering, see Rico, Gabriele Lusser (1983). *Writing the Natural Way: Using Right-Brain Techniques to Release Your Expressive Powers*. Los Angeles: J. P. Tarcher, Inc.

Target Skills: Writing (generating creative ideas through clustering ideas)

Things You'll Need: Model of bubble diagram for each child, white paper, and pencil or pen

Game Plan

1. Talk to the children about free verse poetry, how it doesn't rhyme but has a pleasing sound. Tell them that they will write short free verse poems with the help of a bubble diagram.

2. Make copies of a bubble diagram with a large bubble in the middle and one or more bubbles radiating from the main circle.

3. Distribute the diagrams to the children. The children will write or draw an idea in the diagram's center and then use this idea to inspire them to think of ideas for writing a poem. They will write or dictate these ideas in a brief phrase or picture form in the bubbles that spring from the large bubble.

4. The children will take their diagrams to their homework helpers. With their help, they will compose a poem about the theme (contained in the large bubble), using some of the ideas in the smaller bubbles. They do not have to use all the ideas, only the ones they think fit the poem best.

5. The helpers will write the rough draft as the children dictate it. After revising the rough draft with the helper's assistance, the children can copy (or dictate) the final copy.

6. The children will bring their poems to school and illustrate them.

7. The children (or you) will read their poems to the class and show their pictures. The other students will say why they liked each poem.

Sample Script: "You're going to use this bubble diagram to write your own poem with your homework helper. The poem can be short, and it doesn't have to rhyme. We call a poem that doesn't rhyme *free verse*.

"You'll see a big bubble in the middle of the page. Write or draw a main idea for writing a poem in that circle. Here are some ideas you may want to write about: friends, going out to play, doing something at the seashore or the mountains, going out to a restaurant, or visiting relatives.

"Write or draw some things that these main ideas make you think about in the smaller bubbles. Now you're ready to write or dictate your poem to your homework helper.

"After you finish writing your poem, you'll bring it back to class and draw a picture to illustrate it. You'll read your poems to the class, and the other students will say what they like about each poem."

54. Guess the Verb

Description: Help the child identify verbs and give practice using them in sentences.

Target Skills: Writing (use of action verbs in sentences), speaking, and listening

Things You'll Need: Short picture book, pen, paper, and highlighter

Game Plan

1. Give examples of action verbs. Read a short picture book and ask the class to identify at least one action word on each page.

2. Ask the children to give examples of action verbs. Ask volunteers to demonstrate the action of the verbs the other students name.

3. Have the children take turns acting out verbs while the rest of the class tries to figure out what the action is. Ask why this word is an action verb.

4. Have the class make up a list of verbs and write them on the board. Ask the class to write or dictate sentences for any three of the action verbs, highlighting the verbs.

Sample Script: "Action verbs are types of words that make writing sparkle. Can you give an example of words that express action?" (Suggested answers: *shout*, *laugh*, and *skip*.) "I'm going to read a story. After each page I'll stop and ask you to name at least one action verb on that page. I'd like you to show that action to the class.

"Next, I'll ask you each to think of one action verb and to act out the verbs (for example, *run*, *dance*, *throw*) for the whole group. See if the other children can guess which verb you're acting out.

"After we make a list of the action verbs you act out, you'll write (or dictate) sentences using any action verb from the list. Remember that a sentence needs a complete thought.

"Here is an example of a sentence using an action verb: 'I pet the barking dog.' If I only said, *barking dog*, why wouldn't that be a sentence?" (It doesn't have a complete thought.) "I'd like you to highlight the action verb in each sentence."

55. Predict a Story

Description: Give the child practice in predicting events in a story. The child also makes up original story endings.

Target Skills: Reading, writing, and speaking

Things You'll Need: Longer picture storybooks, paper, and pen

Game Plan

1. Read a longer picture storybook that has a more involved plot than a simple picture book. Stop reading before the story ends. Ask the children to work with a partner to predict the ending in light of what happened in the story.

2. In a brief form, record the different story endings the children suggest. Then read the actual story ending and compare it with what the children suggested.

3. Ask the children to comment on the actual story ending. If the ending is different from theirs, ask if they like that ending or one of theirs better. Have them explain why.

Sample Script: "Today I'm going to read you a picture storybook. This book is longer than a regular picture book. I'll pass around some picture storybooks. How do they look different from a regular picture book?" (They have more pages and more words on the pages.)

"After I read one of these books, I'd like you to work with a partner. I'm going to stop right before the story ends. Please think about how you think the story will end. After I read the end of the story, we'll compare your ending with the author's.

"What did you like or dislike about the author's ending? Did you like someone in the class's ending better? Why?"

56. Hunt for Nouns

Description: Help the child identify and use nouns and adjectives. Give practice in using alliteration (repetition of the initial consonant sound) with adjective and noun combinations.

Target Skills: Writing and speaking

Things You'll Need: Pen and paper

Game Plan

1. Review nouns (persons, places, or things). This activity focuses on things.

2. Explain adjectives. You can call them *describing words* or *adjectives*. Explain that adjectives describe nouns.

3. Ask the children to name objects in the room. Write the nouns on the board.

4. Have the children work as a class to make up sentences about the nouns, using adjectives with the same beginning sounds as the nouns to describe the nouns. They will take turns dictating sentences about the nouns and the adjectives.

5. After you read each sentence, ask the children to identify the nouns and adjectives.

Sample Script: "A noun can be a person, place, or thing. Today we're going to look at some things in this room. I'd like you to name something you see in the room. After I write the names of all the things you think of on the board, I'd like you to think of a describing word to put in front of each of the nouns.

"Make the describing word start with the same beginning sound as the noun (for example, if the noun is *crayons*, you can use the adjective *colorful*). Here are more examples of describing words and nouns that start with the same sound: *puffy pillow, creamy cupcake, blue book, and toy tiger*.

"Then I'd like you to think of sentences with the nouns and the describing words in front of the nouns. Here's an example: 'I drew a picture with the *colorful crayons*.'

"You can tell me the describing word and the noun it tells about after I read each sentence."

57. Choose a Feeling Card

Description: Practice sentence writing by asking the child to complete a sentence about feelings.

Target Skills: Writing, speaking

Things You'll Need: Index cards with a feeling listed on each card, pen, paper, and markers

Game Plan

1. Ask the children to talk about different feelings a person can show. Have them take turns acting out how people show feelings by their words, their facial expressions, and their body language. What does *happy* (*sad, angry, surprised*) look like?

2. Write one feeling (*happy, sad*, etc.) on each index card. Ask each child to choose one card. Have the children write or dictate a sentence for each feeling. If they need help getting started, provide them with prompts to start off each sentence.

3. Have them illustrate their sentences with drawings that reflect the feeling they wrote about. They will write or dictate the name of the feeling beneath the picture.

Sample Script: "Tell me about some feelings people can have."(Suggested answers: happy, surprised, angry, bored, and excited.) "I'd like you to think about how people talk, act, and look when they show different feelings. What do they say? How do their eyes and mouths look? How do they move their bodies?

"These index cards have one feeling written on each card. I'd like each of you to pick a card and act out the feeling for the class. See if the other children can guess the feeling. If you need to, offer a hint. You can say something like, 'When I get a day to play on the beach, I am _____' (happy) or 'I yawn when I am _____' (bored).

"Now I'd like each of you to write or tell me a sentence about the feeling you acted out. Draw a picture of you or someone else showing that feeling. Write (or dictate) the name of the feeling underneath the picture."

58. Make a Scrapbook Poster (Homework Helper Activity)

Description: Give practice in recognizing and using verbs by having the child make a poster about a family member, listing that person's traits and hobbies.

Target Skills: Writing (using verbs) and character development (family appreciation)

Things You'll Need: Construction paper, white paper, markers, crayons, glue stick, glitter or other decorations, and snapshot of family member

Game Plan

1. Discuss *verb phrases*. You can call it "a group of words that be-gins with an action word." Everything except for the subject

(what the sentence is about) is called the *verb phrase*. Give sample verb phrases and have the children give examples.

2. With the aid of the homework helper, the children will make a poster honoring a family member. They will glue the family member's picture on construction paper and write the relative's name under the picture.

3. The children will write or dictate verb phrases (at least two or three) that describe the family member. The homework helper will write the phrases on strips of paper and the children will paste them on the poster. The children will bring the posters to class and will decorate them with designs and glitter.

4. The children will show and explain their scrapbook posters to the class. Later, they will present the scrapbook poster to the family member it honors.

Sample Script: "Do you know what a scrapbook is?" (Words and pictures about some part of your life such as your family, friends, or things you've enjoyed doing.) "I'd like you to work with your homework helper to make a scrapbook poster to honor a family member. You can make your poster about a parent, a brother or sister, a grandparent, aunt, uncle, or anyone you want.

"Your family will give you a picture of your relative, which you can glue onto the paper, or you can draw a picture. I'd like you to think about some words you can use to describe your relative. I'd like you to use a group of words that begin with an action word (verb phrase) to describe your family member. Think of two or three verb phrases to describe the person.

"Here's an example: under your grandmother's picture, you may want to write 'Paints pictures, grows flowers, and works in a dress shop.' You can see that each group of words begins with an action word (verb) and that it tells things about your grandmother. Write (or have your helper write) the group of words starting with the action word on a strip of white paper. You'll then glue it where you think it looks best on your scrapbook poster.

"You'll show the class your scrapbook poster and tell about your family member. Then you'll give it to your relative as a special gift."

59. My, Oh My, It's a Wonderful Day!

Description: Stress organizational skills and written and artistic expression and encourage a positive outlook by making a collage to spark storytelling.

Target Skills: Writing, speaking, organizational skills, and character development (self-reliance)

Things You'll Need: Old magazines (preferably children's magazines), large poster board, scissors, and glue stick

Game Plan

1. The children brainstorm ideas with a partner about the little things that make a day happy (family, friends, playing with a favorite toy or game, learning new things, going on day trips, etc.).

2. The partners cut out pictures representing things they find enjoyable and glue them in an attractive form onto poster board. They dictate or write the name of the activity on a slip of paper and glue it near the corresponding picture.

3. Ask the partners to tell the story of a wonderful day in words that relate to the pictures they chose.

4. Close the activity by asking the class, "What makes your day happy?"

Sample Script: "What kinds of things make your day happy? Suppose you're feeling tired or a little sad, what kinds of things cheer you up?

"I'd like you and a partner to think about the things that make a wonderful day. Look through these magazines and cut out pictures of people enjoying their day or of things that make them happy.

"Paste the pictures any way you want on the construction paper. When you make them touch one another and arrange them in an attractive way, we call it a *collage*. Write (or dictate) on strips of paper the words that describe the pictures. Then you'll glue the words near the pictures.

"You and your partner will tell us a story about the pictures and words you chose. Then we're going to talk more about what makes you have a wonderful day."

INTERMEDIATE

6 0. "All the World's a Stage"

Description: Encourage creative play and advance writing and speaking abilities by using puppets to write and act out a short skit about how to solve a problem.

Target Skills: Writing, speaking, outlining, and character development (problem solving)

Things You'll Need: Finger puppets or socks and markers to make them, chairs, blanket or sheet or any type of stage, pen, and paper

Game Plan

1. Brainstorm problem situations that the children might face during their day. Ask partners or small groups to think of possible solutions to the problems. Take notes on the whole class discussion after the partners or groups discuss them.

2. Ask partners or groups to write short skits about a problem and how they might solve it.

3. Provide finger puppets or ask the children to make puppets with socks. (They can draw faces and hair on the socks with markers.)

4. Have the children plan their plays by discussing their ideas for the plot with their partners or groups. You can write down their ideas in a brief outline form, and they will refer to them (with your help) if they need help plotting their plays. They

can practice their plays using the ideas as a guide for plotting the events. (Instead of writing a scripted play, they will plan out the main events and ad-lib the lines.)

5. The partners or groups will perform their plays. The audience will ask the characters (puppets) in the play to answer questions related to the story line.

Sample Script: "You're going to write short plays called *skits* about solving a problem. Can you think of some problems you've had or ones you've seen other children dealing with?" (Possible answers: someone being unkind to another person, someone not sharing, someone who wants another child's toy, or someone not listening to a parent or teacher.)

"You can make your own puppets for the play with socks and markers or you can use these finger puppets. Let's think of some ideas for a stage (a sheet over a couple of chairs, for example).

"Next you'll talk about ideas to put in your play. I can help by writing an outline of what you want your play to be about. Just like a story, your skit should have a beginning, middle, and end. First show what the problem is by having the puppets talk about it. Then show what happens because of the problem. At the end, find a way to solve the problem.

"Once you know what you want the play to be about, you can think of lines to say that go with the ideas you wrote. After you practice your play with your partner or group, you'll perform it for the class.

"After you put on your play, someone may want to ask the characters questions about the play or may want to talk about more ways to solve the problem in the play."

61. What Kind of Sound Does an Aardvark Make?

Description: Sharpen descriptive powers and help the child make inferences about sounds animals make, based on research, using a children's picture dictionary, books, and the Internet.

Target Skills: Reading, vocabulary, speaking, research, and making inferences

Things You'll Need: A child's picture dictionary, books about animals, and websites for children about animals

Game Plan

1. Ask the children to make sounds that pets or animals they've seen in the zoo make. Have them describe the sounds using one or two words. Ask them to take turns imitating the animals using motions and body language.

2. Help the children (working with partners) research an animal that interests them, focusing on the animal's habits and sounds.

3. Have the children tell the class about the animal they chose and what they and their partners learned. Ask the class to vote on the most interesting animal and to tell why.

Sample Script: "Let's talk about the kinds of sounds different animals make. Can you name some animals you've seen in the zoo or ones that you have as pets and imitate their sounds? Think of one word to describe that sound. Can you also imitate how that animal moves?

"Now that we've talked about the animals you've seen or have as pets, we're going to look in these books and on the Internet to learn more about other animals. I'd like you and a partner to choose one animal you'd like to learn more about.

"Think of these questions when you study the animal: What kind of sounds does the animal make? What does the animal eat? What does it like to do? Is it friendly to other types of animals? In what parts of the world would you find the animal? Would the animal make a good pet? Why or why not?

"After you tell the class about the animal you and your partner studied, they will vote on the animal they'd most want to meet and tell why."

62. Who Am I?

Description: Give practice in speaking and writing by using a book, movie, sports figure, or cartoon character's speech, language, and mannerisms to play a guessing game.

Target Skills: Speaking, writing (use of description), and listening

Things You'll Need: Poster board and pen

Game Plan

1. Ask the children to think of a famous person or fictional character. Have them take turns imitating the character's speech and mannerisms without the use of props.

2. Ask class members to guess the character. If they need help, the person imitating the character will give them verbal clues.

3. Have the class dictate at least three descriptive words (adjectives) that describe each famous character the students imitated. Students will take turns composing sentences using one of the adjectives to describe the characters.

4. Display a poster listing all of the words used to describe the characters. Twice a week ask the children to use one of the describing words in a sentence.

Sample Script: "Think of a person, a real one, or one you've read about or seen in books, movies, or cartoons. Think about how he or she talks, moves, and acts, and pretend to be that person. We'll try to guess who the person is by the way you talk and act. If no one guesses the character, you can give clues." (Example: I wear big rimmed glasses and have a mop of hair—Harry Potter.)

"After someone figures out who the character is, I'd like all of you to think of three describing words (adjectives) to use to tell about the character. Then tell me a sentence about the person using one of the describing words.

"We'll make a list of all describing words and hang it on the wall. Twice a week, you'll write sentences using a describing word from the list."

63. Welcome to My Neighborhood

Description: Give the child the experience of composing plays using toy figures while focusing on how polite behavior affects peoples' lives.

Target Skills: Writing, speaking, and character development (polite behavior)

Things You'll Need: Blocks, toy people figures or homemade ones, pen and paper

Game Plan

1. Ask the children to think of some things people say and do to show they are polite. Ask how this makes other people act toward them in return. Make a list on the board as the children name ways that people show courteous behavior.

2. Provide toy people figures and blocks to create a neighborhood (either the one they live in or an imaginary one such as a kingdom with kings and queens). The children work with a partner to write a short play that deals with ways they can show polite behavior.

3. While creating their plays, the children will also focus on the reaction of other people to the polite behavior. The partners will stage their plays for the class, and the audience will identify the polite behavior addressed in each play.

4. The children will make an effort to show courteous behavior on a daily basis. Give small rewards such as stars and stickers as this occurs.

Sample Script: "Can you tell me some things people say and do to show they're polite?" (For example, say *please, thank you,* and *excuse me*; hold the door open for the next person; or pick up something a person drops.)

"When you are polite to people, how does this affect the way they act toward you?" (Possible answer: They act more polite; they listen to me; and they like to be around me.)

"You and your partner are going to write a short play about things you can say and do to show courtesy to other people. Also, show how they might act after you've been polite to them. You can use these toy people or make your own. Make a neighborhood for the people to live in with these blocks. Make your neighborhood the one you live in, or make it a pretend kingdom with kings and queens.

"You'll perform your plays for the class. Then every time I see you being polite, I'll paste a star or sticker on your chart. But what do you think the main reward will be?" (Possible response: I'll feel happy. People will be kinder to me.)

64. Solve the Secret Clues

Description: Help the child learn to follow directions by following a trail of clues to find a surprise. Build reading comprehension skills.

Target Skills: Reading and following directions

Things You'll Need: A supply of short riddles that you've prepared in advance (with picture clues of the objects), notes to leave at different checkpoints, familiar objects to hide, and small gifts

Game Plan

1. Have the children work with one or more other children. Provide a supply (three or four) of short rhymed or unrhymed riddles at different checkpoints. Each riddle gives a clue, which leads the children closer to an object.

2. Draw picture clues on all parts of the riddles and read the clues to explain them. Tell the students ahead of time what objects they're trying to find. Provide help for those who need it by reading the clues.

3. The children follow each clue on the journey to find the hidden objects.

4. Whoever finds an object first wins a prize. Provide small prizes to the entire group for participating in the activity and for trying their best.

Sample Script: "We're going to play 'Solve the Secret Clues' using clues to find hidden objects. I'm going to read you the clues, but there are also pictures of the clues to help you know where to go next. If you need me to read a clue, raise your hand.

"Here are some examples of clues: Clue 1: Look near a stuffed bear under a chair; Clue 2: Under the big clock, look for a clue in a block; Clue 3: Next to a storybook is the next place to look; You've found the stuffed dog! Good job!

"Let's see who can follow the clues and find the (truck, stuffed dog, watch) first. Whoever finds one of the objects first wins."

65. Deviled Eggs and Brownie Pie

Description: Build sensory awareness, descriptive powers, and speaking ability by staging a TV cooking show.

Target Skills: Speaking, listening, vocabulary development, descriptive ability, and following directions

Things You'll Need: Toy oven (or a homemade one), toy stove (or a homemade one), groceries (canned goods and empty containers or cartons), toy or real vegetables, plastic dishes, pots, pans, and utensils

Game Plan

1. Have the children work with a partner and take turns pretending they're TV chefs. First they will figure out which meal they want to cook and then practice being on-camera chefs.

2. Tell them to prepare a breakfast, lunch, or dinner they'd enjoy eating. Ask them to show the group how to prepare a simple dish (soup, baked potato, or grilled cheese).

3. They should describe the process as they "cook" the food. Is the food cooked on top of the stove or in the oven? How long should it cook? Does it need to be stirred or turned over? Ask the partners to tell the types and quantities of ingredients and to tell how certain seasonings or a lack of them will affect the taste of the food.

4. Have them describe colors, aromas, and textures of the finished foods.

5. Ask partners to conclude their show by describing their favorite foods.

Sample Script: "You're going to take turns pretending you're TV chefs. You and your partner will pretend to cook a breakfast, lunch, or dinner on this toy stove. Don't forget dessert and what you'll have to drink. Here are some different foods and pots and pans.

"As you cook, tell the audience (the class) what you need to do to cook the food. Think about what will happen if you don't cook it long enough or if you leave it on the stove for too long. Talk about the ingredients you'll need and how much of each ingredient you'll need. Will you use any seasonings in the food? How will seasonings change the taste of the food?

"After you explain how to cook the food, I'd like you to describe the colors and smells of the food. How does the food feel if you touch it? (soft, hard, mushy, or fluffy) What is your favorite food? Describe it."

66. Step into a Story (Homework Helper Activity)

Description: Encourage a love of reading and make a book come alive for the child by making reading an interactive experience. The child writes a story based on a favorite character.

Target Skills: Reading, writing, speaking, and listening

Things You'll Need: Picture book or picture storybooks chosen by the children and writing materials

Game Plan

1. Ask the children to vote on favorite books that you have available. Have them choose one with a character they find appealing.

2. Before you read the book, ask the children to think of a few questions they can ask about the main character that will help them get inside the character. Write the questions as the children brainstorm. Explain that after they hear the story and answer their questions as a class, they'll read another story of their choice with their homework helpers. Then they'll dictate or write their own story about the main character.

3. Read the story and have the children discuss the character, using their questions as a guideline.

4. After the homework helpers read a favorite story the children choose, the children will write or dictate their own stories about the main character. The homework helper will use the questions in the sample script below as a guideline for writing the story.

5. The children will bring their stories to class and tell or read them to the group.

Sample Script: "I'm going to give the titles of some stories we've read that you've enjoyed. You're going to vote on your favorite one. After you choose a story, I'll ask you to think of a few questions you can ask to help you learn about the main person in the story. Then you'll read another story and write your own story about the main character with your homework helper.

"Here are some sample questions to get you started: If you were the main person in the story, what would you wear? How would you comb your hair? How would you talk? Would you be shy or talk a lot? Would you have a lot of friends or just a few? If a problem came up, what would you do? I'd like you to think of your own questions too. I'll write them down and we'll come back to them before you write your story.

"Now that I've read the story and we've talked about the character using your questions, it's time to write (or tell) your homework helper your own story. Your homework helper will read you a favorite book. Try making the main person in the story have a different adventure than the one in the story your helper reads to you.

"After you write your story with your helper, you can read or tell it to everyone here."

67. Scentsations (Homework Helper Activity)

Description: Sharpen sensory awareness by awakening the senses of smell and taste. Show cause and effect relationships and strengthen critical thinking skills.

Target Skills: Writing (powers of observation and description) and making comparisons

Things You'll Need: A variety of spices (fresh and/or dried) and flavorings (such as pure vanilla, chocolate, and strawberry sauce) displayed on a table, small plastic spoons, and writing materials

Game Plan

1. Set up a variety of spices and flavorings on a table. Label each one. Ask the children to take turns smelling and tasting each one and to describe its scent and flavor.

2. Have the children write (or dictate) on a chart labeled with each spice how each one smelled and/or tasted to them.

3. Have children work with partners and think about what type of food each spice or flavoring would complement. How would it make it taste different or better?

4. Ask the partners to compare the smell and taste of each item to something they've smelled or tasted before.

5. Ask the children to try at least one of the spices or seasonings sampled in class at home and report back to the class about how it changed the taste when added to one or more foods.

Sample Script: "When you think about how to describe things, it makes you see things more clearly. When writers make up stories, they think about how to describe things and people so that we can picture them.

97

"Today you're going to smell and taste different seasonings and flavorings. Your family probably uses some of these spices and flavorings when they make dinners or desserts, so you may know about them already.

"We're going to make a chart and I'll write what you say about how each spice or flavoring smells and tastes. Then you'll work with a partner and tell me how each spice or flavoring would make food taste different or better than it does now.

"When you smell the spice or flavoring, ask yourself if it smells like a flower or strong coffee. Does it taste bitter like a grapefruit or sweet like a strawberry?

"Ask your family if you can try out some of the spices and flavorings we worked with today and let us know how the spice or flavoring changed the taste of the food." (Possible answer: The garlic powder smelled strong and tasted a little bitter. It made the garlic bread taste spicy. The chocolate syrup tasted sweet but not as sweet as hot fudge. It made the vanilla ice cream taste like I melted a candy bar over it.)

"At home, you can also try adding a little or a lot of the spice or flavoring to the food. Tell the class if it tastes just right or too hot and spicy if you add a lot or a little seasoning or flavoring."

68. You're a Poet and You Know It

Description: Build creativity and writing skills by having the class write short free verse poems about nature.

Target Skills: Writing, use of verbs and adjectives in writing and speaking

Things You'll Need: Markers and poster board

Game Plan

1. Ask the children to list beautiful sights in nature. Ask them to list describing words (adjectives) that they would use to describe these things. Also ask them to list verbs (action words) they might use with the topics they chose. Copy their ideas as they dictate a list of adjectives and verbs.

2. As a class, they will write a short poem using these adjectives and verbs to write short (four to six lines) free verse poems about something beautiful in nature.

3. As the children think of ideas for the poems, write them on the board. Then ask them to revise the poems as a class. Copy the final versions on large poster boards.

4. All students will take turns drawing illustrations for the poems on the poster board. Display poems for visitors.

Sample Script: "Think of something beautiful in nature that you like to see like the sun, a rainbow, snow, or flowers. We will decide upon a topic and write a short poem and draw a picture about it as a class.

"First, we'll make a list of describing words for each thing you mention. We'll also list some verbs or action words you can use in the poem. You'll dictate some describing words and action verbs that you can use with your idea for a poem. I'll write the describing words and action words under the subject you'll write about.

"Say you decide to write a poem about the sun. Here are some describing words you can use in a poem about the sun: *yellow* and *orange*. Here are some action words: *blinks* and *fades*. You don't have to use all of the describing and action words in the poem, only the ones that fit best.

"After we make our lists, you'll work as a class to write free verse poems about things you've admired in nature. Once you think of the lines for your poem, we'll make it sound better by making a few changes in the words or the rhythm of the poem.

"Each poem will have four to six lines and it will be a free verse poem. A free verse poem doesn't rhyme, but the words combine to make a pleasant sound. There's an example on the board of a short free verse poem about the sun:

> The yellow sun blinks in the sky.
> I see it through my window.
> The orange sunset fades into the sky.
> I say good-bye to another day.

Here's another free verse poem about a butterfly:

> I saw a butterfly land on a flower.
> It had colors like a paint set—
> red, yellow, and blue.
> It landed on my hand and flew away.

After you write your poems, you'll take turns drawing pictures on the poster board to decorate the poems. When people come to visit, you'll show them your poems."

69. Willy Nilly, Shilly Shally

Description: Pair rhyming words or words beginning with the same consonant (alliteration) to achieve different sound effects. Show how words have a melody and create mood in speaking and writing.

Target Skills: Writing (rhyming, alliteration), speaking, and listening

Things You'll Need: Pen, paper, and small prizes

Game Plan

1. The children take turns pairing rhyming one- and two-syllable words (they can also rhyme first names) and words that start with the same consonant sound. The words that start with the same consonant sound don't have to rhyme. The students may also use nonsense words in both games.

2. The last person left in the rhyming contest wins a small prize. Also, give a prize for the silliest rhyme or first letter sound, according to children's votes.

Sample Script: "Today we're going to play a rhyming game with words you use every day and also with first names. You'll say a word and then give a word that rhymes with it. Each person will take a turn. The last person left in the game that gives the most rhyming words wins the game. The words can be regular words or silly words you make up.

"Here are some words that rhyme: *clock, sock*; *toy, soy*; *sheep, peep*; and *willy, nilly.* You can use names too: *Andy, candy*; *slim, Jim*; *Lisa, geesa.* You can rhyme the names with real words or silly words.

"We'll also play a game with words that start with the same sound. These words don't have to rhyme. Here are some words that start with the same sound that don't rhyme: *shilly shally*; *quick quack*; *barking bulldog*; *lucky Linda*; and *smiling Sara.*

"The last person left in the contest wins. You'll also vote on the silliest rhyme pair or first letter sound."

70. Word Workout

Description: Build vocabulary and practice using synonyms and adjectives to describe objects.

Target Skills: Writing (synonyms, describing skills), speaking, and vocabulary development

Things You'll Need: Objects found at home or in school such as stuffed toys, jewelry, plastic containers, kitchen utensils, dolls, toy cars, and common foods

Game Plan

1. Place some objects such as those listed above on the table or floor. Ask the children to take turns naming the objects and to think of different words for the same object (synonyms).

2. Write the synonyms for each object as the children dictate them.

3. Have the children dictate sentences about each of the objects, using at least one synonym on the list to describe each object. Write the sentences on the board.

4. Related Activity: Ask the children to take turns examining the objects you assembled for the last activity. Ask them to think of describing words (adjectives) for each object. Make a list of

describing words and have them compose a sentence using each one.

Sample Script: "I'd like you to take turns looking at these things on the table and name them. Then think of another name for each object. You'll think of as many words as you can for the same object. Here are some ideas: *toy bear* (stuffed animal, teddy bear); *necklace* (beads, jewelry); and *sweets* (candy, cake, cookies). I'll write the words for the objects down as you say them. Then you'll tell me a sentence for each synonym and I'll write it on the board.

"We're going to look at these objects again. This time I'd like you to think of some describing words (adjectives) for each thing you see. Here are some examples of describing words for the objects: *toy bear* (soft, cuddly, warm); *necklace* (shiny, silver, bright); and *sweets* (sugary, syrupy).

"We're going to make a list of all your describing words. Then you'll tell me a sentence using the describing word and the object you see."

71. Build a Story with Verbs

Description: Increase vocabulary and help the child identify verbs and give synonyms for verbs by viewing the pictures in a storybook.

Target Skills: Reading, writing, speaking, vocabulary building, and listening

Things You'll Need: Picture book with a lot of action, pen and paper

Game Plan

1. Read a favorite picture book. After discussing the story, show the children the pictures, and ask them to raise their hands when they see a picture that shows action.

2. Ask the children to take turns giving one action word to describe what the characters are doing in the picture. Have volunteers imitate the action in the picture. Ask who can think of another verb to describe the same action.

3. Make a list of all the verbs and ask the group to dictate a collective story (six to eight sentences) using at least five of the verbs.

Sample Script: "I'm going to read a picture book that has a lot of action going on. After I read the book, I'm going to show you the pictures one by one. Raise your hand when you see a picture of a person (or an animal) doing something. An action word is called a *verb*. I'd like you to tell me an action word for each picture.

"After you tell me the action word, I'll ask for a volunteer to imitate the action in the story. I'll make a list of all the action words you tell me.

"After we complete our list, I'd like you to think of other words (synonyms) that you could use in place of the action words you gave (synonyms). Here are some examples: *run* (race, dash, rush); *laugh* (chuckle, giggle); and *eat* (gobble, swallow, gulp down). Next, you're going to write a story as a class, using at least five of the verbs or synonyms."

72. Tell Me a Story Again!

Description: Reinforce writing skills and help the child understand story structure by having him or her tell a story.

Target Skills: Writing and speaking

Things You'll Need: Picture book, picture storybook, or simple chapter book

Game Plan

1. After you've read a favorite story, let the children take turns telling you the story in their own words.

2. Have the children take turns continuing the story where the previous child left off. Prompt the child telling the story by asking questions like these: Tell about the main character. What happened when _____? Why was this an important part of the story? What did the character do when _____? How did the main character solve the problem? If you were the author, how would you have ended the story?

3. Make the children aware of story structure by asking what happened in the beginning, middle, and end of the story.

4. Ask if they like the way the story ended. If not, how would they like to see it end?

Sample Script: "I'm going to read you a story. After I finish, I'm going to ask what happened in different parts of the story. There are three parts to a story: the beginning, middle, and end.

"You're going to take turns telling the story. When I ask one of you to stop, the next person will take a turn telling what happens until we get to the last person. That person will tell the end of the story.

"I'd like you to think about the way the story ends. Did you like the ending? If you didn't, how would you like to see the story end?"

73. Clap a Mini Poem (Homework Helper Activity)

Description: Emphasize the rhythm of poetry by clapping out the beat of a poem. Develop creative writing skills.

Target Skills: Reading, writing, speaking, and listening

Things You'll Need: Children's poetry collection of your choice, pen and paper

Game Plan

1. Talk about how poetry, like music, has its own melody.

2. Read rhymed poems from a children's book of poetry. Choose short poems on child-pleasing topics.

3. Explain how poetry has a regular beat that sounds like good music. Read the poem a second time and clap out the beat. Read it a third time and have children clap out the poem with you. To minimize noise, children can clap their laps.

4. As a follow-up, ask the class to write or dictate a two-lined rhymed poem. Have them recite the poem and clap out the beat with the class on the second reading.

5. Have the children dictate a two-line mini poem to their homework helpers. Have them explain to the helpers how to clap out a poem. The children and helpers will clap out the poem together. The children will bring the mini poems they wrote to class and you will read them aloud.

Sample Script: "Why do you like to hear poetry?" (Possible answers: because I like how it sounds; it's fun to hear the stories poems tell.) "Poems have a rhythm of their own, like music, so they're pleasant to read and hear.

"I'm going to read poems from this children's book of poetry. I'd like you to listen to the rhythm of the poems and to think about how the words sound pleasant like music. I'll read the poem a second time and clap out the beat. I'll read it a third time and you can clap out the beat of the poem on your laps like this.

"After we read and clap out our poems as a class, you're going to write or tell me a short poem that has a rhyme at the end of each line. Each poem will have two lines. Here are some examples of mini poems:

> I like to play
> at school each day.

> My cat caught a mouse
> Hiding in my house.

> I had a dream
> I ate ice cream.

The class will clap out your poem the second time we read it. Sometimes poems change the beat rather than keep the same beat. Why do you think that is?" (Possible answer: to make the poem more interesting or to surprise the reader.)

"Next, you will write a mini poem like the one you wrote in class with your homework helper. After you think about your poem, you will dictate it to your helper. See if you like the way the poem sounds or if you want to change anything before you bring your poem to class.

"Explain to your helper how to clap out a poem. Together, you can clap out the poem you wrote. Bring in the poem you wrote, and I'll read it to the class."

74. Build a Word Combo

Description: Teach nouns and the adjectives that describe them and progress to sentence building by working with word combinations.

Target Skills: Writing and speaking

Things You'll Need: Pen, paper, and markers

Game Plan

1. Ask the children to brainstorm a list of nouns (persons, places, or things). Write the nouns on the board.

2. Working with partners, have the children think of a describing word (adjective) to describe each noun. Write the word combinations on the board as the children dictate them.

3. After the partners write word combinations (noun preceded by an adjective), ask the class to think of sentences using the word combinations.

4. Next, have the children write or dictate one of their own sentences, using one of the word combinations, and write them on construction paper. Children will illustrate their sentence with markers.

Sample Script: "A noun is any person, place, or thing. Let's see if you can name some nouns. I'll write them as you say them.

"If we put describing words in front of a noun, we'll learn more about the noun. Here are some nouns and describing words: funny *clown* (person), crowded *mall* (place), salty *popcorn* (thing).

"I'd like you and your partner to make a word combination with a noun and a describing word in front of the noun. Think of describing words that tell about any of the nouns on the list we made. The word *the* can also be a describing word, but I'd like you to think of words like the ones I gave you that actually describe the noun.

"Now that you've thought of your word combinations, I'll say and write them. Everyone will think of one sentence using one of the word combinations you made up.

"Then you will write or dictate your sentence and draw a picture showing the sentence you wrote. Here are some sentence examples using the word combinations I gave you:

The *funny clown* juggled the bottles.
The *crowded mall* has a large food court.
The *salty popcorn* made me thirsty.

"Let your sentence start with the word *the* and any word combination we talked about."

75. E-mail a Family Member (Homework Helper Activity)

Description: Practice writing vivid descriptions and using logical thought progression in writing by sending an e-mail to a relative.

Target Skills: Writing, organizing, and character development (family closeness)

Things You'll Need: Home or school computer access, pen and paper

Game Plan

1. This is a home/school project. The children will organize their e-mails in school and will write their e-mails with the help of a family member on a home computer.

2. Help the children organize their thoughts in an outline by discussing what they're going to write in an e-mail to a family

member. They will dictate or write a brief list of ideas to help them organize their e-mails.

3. Give the children ideas by asking guiding questions about what they're doing lately that might interest a relative.

4. After they write their e-mails at home, ask them to make a copy of the responses they receive and to share them with the class.

Sample Script: "Everyone is going to send a family member an e-mail. You may want to write to a grandparent, an aunt, uncle, or cousin. First, we're going to write some ideas about what you're going to talk about in your e-mail. An outline will help you put your e-mail together so that it makes good sense.

"Think of the things your family member would like to hear. Here are some questions to help you think about what you'll write (or dictate) in your outline:

> What is the most interesting new thing you've learned at home or in school?
> What have you done lately that you enjoyed?
> What interesting place did you visit?
> What questions would you like to ask your family member?

Ask your homework helper to help you write the e-mail to your family member. When the person writes back, please print out the e-mail and you can read it, or tell us about what the family member wrote to you."

76. Family Picture Album (Homework Helper Activity)

Description: Teach descriptive writing by helping the child write descriptive sentences around the drawing of a family member.

Target Skills: Writing (descriptive), speaking, and character development (family closeness)

Things You'll Need: Pen, paper, glue stick, white and construction paper

Game Plan

1. The homework helpers will assist the children in drawing a picture of a relative, and the children will bring the pictures to school. They can draw the picture from memory or from looking at the person or a picture.

2. At home the children will dictate or write a list of adjectives that describe the person in the picture. Using the adjectives they listed, the children will dictate or write one or two sentences about their family member. The homework helper will write the sentences on small strips of white paper.

3. The children will bring in the sentences and the pictures. They will mount the pictures on construction paper and will arrange their sentences around the picture in an interesting pattern.

4. Have them show and talk about their picture albums to the class. The students will then give their projects to the family member about whom they wrote.

Sample Script: "I'd like you to choose a family member you'd like to write about and draw. You can tell your homework helper some words you'd use to describe the family member whose picture you drew. Then, using the describing words you thought of, you can write (or dictate) one or two sentences about the family member on strips of white paper.

"In a couple of days, you'll bring in the pictures you drew along with your sentences. You'll paste the sentence on the construction paper with your picture. After you finish making your albums, you'll talk about them and show them to the class. Then you can take them home and give them to the person you wrote about as a present."

77. Honor an American Hero (Homework Helper Activity)

Description: Read about and discuss an American hero and write about the person's contributions in a journal.

Target Skills: Reading, writing, speaking, and character development (positive role models)

Things You'll Need: Internet sites and children's nonfiction books dealing with American heroes and copy of journal guideline questions in sample script

Game Plan

1. Read and discuss information from websites and children's nonfiction books on the topic of American heroes.

2. After you read and discuss information about various heroes, discuss the heroes' lives and accomplishments with the class. With the help of a homework helper, children will write or dictate short journal entries (four or five over a two-week period) in the first person, pretending they are the actual heroes. In the journal, they will focus on challenges the hero has faced and overcome.

3. In a time period that you decide, children will bring in journal entries for you or them to read to the class. Ask the children why each person could be called a hero. Is a hero someone who saves someone's life, or could a hero be someone who helps people in a different way?

Sample Script: "What kind of person could be called a hero?" (Possible answers: a person who saves a life; someone who does something very brave; a person who isn't afraid of anything; or someone who helps someone without caring if anyone knows.)

"We're going to look at these books and websites about heroes, and then we'll talk about the things the heroes did to help people. You'll think about which hero you'd like to write a journal about with your homework helper.

"You will pretend you're the hero and will write your journal using *I* instead of *he* or *she*. That will make it seem as if the hero is actually writing.

"Here are some questions to think about as you write your journal. Remember that you are pretending that you are the hero when you write, so the questions are questions for him or her. If you can't answer some of the questions, you can make up your own to fit the person you're writing about.

1. Think about three interesting facts about your life.

2. What kind of work did I do? What were my hobbies or interests?

3. What was a big problem I faced in my life?

4. What did I do to solve the problem?

5. What did I do to help people?

When you finish your journal, you will bring it to class and I'll read it aloud. We'll read a few journals, and we'll talk about what you think makes somebody a hero."

78. Add Color to Sentences (Homework Helper Activity)

Description: Develop observation skills and give writing practice while having the child write a story using questions about colors as prompts.

Target Skills: Writing, speaking, and following directions

Things You'll Need: Supplies to make a booklet, pens, and prepared questions to answer about colors

Game Plan

1. Fold a paper in two to make a three-page booklet for each child. (Reserve the first page for a cover.) Ask the children to take the booklets home. At home the child will choose three colors from a variety of crayon or marker colors.

2. The children will draw a picture on each page using one of the colors chosen.

3. Next to each picture, the children will write or dictate to the homework helper two sentences about each of the colors in response to the prompts on the sheet you provided to the homework helper. The children will decorate the covers and will give their color booklets a title.

4. The children will show their booklets to classmates and tell why they chose the colors they did.

Sample Script: "When you go home, you're going to choose three different crayons or markers. Using one of your favorite colors, draw a picture on each page of the booklet I gave you. Your homework helper will help you write two sentences about each color you used in drawing your pictures. Draw a cover on the first page, and give the booklet an interesting title.

"Remember that a sentence is a complete thought. Who can give me an example of a sentence?

"Here are some questions about the colors to help you write your sentences. Choose two questions to answer in two sentences for each page in your booklet. Use two different questions for each picture.

1. Why do you like the color?

2. What does the color make you think of?

3. Where have you seen that color besides your picture?

4. What color is most like the color you chose?

5. Where have you seen that color in nature?

6. If you could think of one word to describe the color, what would it be?"

79. Which Book Is Best?

Description: Encourage the child to choose books based on personal interests. Build reading comprehension skills and give practice in paraphrasing stories.

Target Skills: Speaking and paraphrasing stories

Things You'll Need: Picture storybooks or chapter books

Game Plan

1. Each day put ten to twelve picture storybooks or chapter books on a table. Tell the children to take a few minutes to look at each book, choosing one which most appeals to them. Ask them to tell why they chose the book they did.

2. Write the names of the books they choose on strips of paper and mix up the papers in a bag. Have the children take turns reaching into the bag to choose a book to read each day for the next few days.

3. After you've finished reading a story, ask the students to take turns telling the stories in their own words. Let each child tell a little of the story and have the next child continue until you reach the end. Give prompts, if necessary, to help the children tell the story chronologically.

4. After the children have paraphrased all the books, have them vote on their favorite story. Ask what made that book stand out among the rest.

Sample Script: "I've set out a few books on this table for you to look over. When you have a chance, look at each book, especially its cover and pictures, and decide which ones you'd like me to read over the next few days.

"I'd like you to take turns telling me about the books in your own words. Tell the story in the order the author tells it. After you've retold all the stories, you'll vote on your favorite book.

"Here are some things to think about when choosing your favorite book: What did you think of the main character? What were the other characters like? Did the story make you want to read more? How did the main character solve the problem in the story? Did you like how the story ended? Would you read another book by this author?"

8⓪. **Make a Safety Booklet**

Description: Enhance speaking and writing skills by discussing aspects of safety that the child encounters. Help the child create a booklet with suggestions for keeping safe in different situations.

Target Skills: Speaking, writing, and Internet and book sources for children's safety information

Things You'll Need: Paper, pen, markers, construction paper, old magazines, and glue stick

Game Plan

1. Research Internet and book information about safety (involving home, school, and neighborhood) for preschoolers. Discuss safety in these three areas with the class.

2. Have the children work with partners to make booklets about safety in everyday life. They will cut out or draw pictures of the different locations (home, school, and neighborhood) in which it's important for them to be aware of safety issues.

3. Have the children write or dictate two sentences each for observing safety practices in the areas of home, school, and neighborhood. They will also dictate a title for the cover.

4. Have them show the class their safety booklets and tell or read their safety tips.

Sample Script: "Can you think of ways you can keep safe at home, in school, and in your neighborhood?" (**Ideas for home safety:** Don't run on wet floors; be sure pot handles are turned toward the stove when helping cook; don't run near glass doors; and be sure water in the faucet is warm, but not too hot, when you use it. **School safety:** Handle scissors carefully and use blunt scissors; don't push or shove others; and don't share drinks from the same glass. **Neighborhood safety**: Don't talk to people you don't know; cross the street with the green light; and don't fight in the car.)

"You're going to work with a partner to make booklets about safety. You can cut out pictures that show different places you'll need to think about safety. Then you can paste them onto the booklets. You'll make one page for home, one for school, and one for the neighborhood.

"You'll write (or dictate) two sentences each, telling what you'll do to keep safe in these three places. You'll write a total of six sentences.

"Give your safety booklet a title, and I will write it on the cover. Then you can show everyone your safety booklet and tell them how to keep safe at home, in school, and in your neighborhood."

ADVANCED

81. Fly a Kite in Three Easy Steps (Homework Helper Activity)

Description: Heighten speaking and writing skills by having the child list the directions for playing a game or doing something enjoyable.

Target Skills: Speaking, writing, and following directions

Things You'll Need: Paper, pen, and markers

Game Plan

1. The children will give examples of how they would give directions for playing a game or doing something fun such as flying a kite.

2. Talk to the class about how to give directions for an activity one step at a time so that the person reading or hearing them can understand them.

3. With the assistance of their homework helpers, the children will create a flier (one page folded) giving directions for playing a game or doing something they enjoy. They will dictate or write simple instructions in a logical order.

4. After they complete their fliers, children will show them to the class and demonstrate their activities and tell the class their directions. They will answer questions from the class.

Sample Script: "Can anyone tell me step-by-step how you would do something you enjoy? If you know the steps in doing something, you can teach someone else to do it.

"Here are some activities you can write directions for: making something in the kitchen like chocolate-covered pretzels, salad, or a grilled cheese sandwich; playing a sport like baseball, basketball, or hockey; enjoying an activity like flying a kite, building a sand castle, making up a play, or putting on a talent show with friends.

"You're going to make a flier listing the steps for your activity. A flier is a piece of paper folded in two. First, you'll think about the things you have to do. Then your homework helper will help you write the steps people need to know to do the activity. Put these steps in an order that everyone can understand.

"You'll draw a picture of the activity on the flier's cover and write the name of the activity under the picture.

"Bring in your flyer and show it to the class. Explain the steps you need to take to do the activity. After the class hears your directions, they should be able to do the activity themselves. The class will have time to ask questions about your directions."

82. Create Your Own Picture Book (Homework Helper Activity)

Description: Reinforce creative writing skills by discussing true-life events to spark a nonfiction story.

Target Skills: Writing, speaking, and listening

Things You'll Need: Magazines, glue sticks, markers, pen, paper, and construction paper for cover

Game Plan

1. Tell the children they are going to create their own picture books and that the books will be nonfiction. Explain that a fiction story is something the author made up, while nonfiction actually happened.

2. Ask the children to talk about an experience they've had (a book they've read, someone they've seen, or something they want to learn more about) that they'd like to write about. Tell them to give examples of why they enjoyed the experience. Tell them that the story needs a beginning, middle, and end, just like a fiction story. They will give their stories an interesting title based upon the books' content.

3. The children will write or dictate their nonfiction stories to their homework helpers and will bring the completed books to class. They will illustrate them in class with drawings or pictures they cut out from magazines and will decorate the covers.

4. Students will share their nonfiction books with the class.

Sample Script: "You're going to write your own picture books with your homework helper. A lot of the books we've read are fiction, stories that the author thought of, but your book will be nonfiction, a true story about you.

"First we'll talk about some ideas for stories. Here are some questions to think about when planning your story: Where did I go that I'd like to tell about? What book did I read that I'd like to recommend? Who did I see that I haven't seen in a while? What did I learn that I want to learn more about?

"You can use the ideas we talked about or you can think of your own ideas. Once you have your story ideas, you can think of the order you want to put the ideas in so that it reads like a good book. You'll want to have a beginning that makes people want to hear more; a middle of the story that tells more about what happens; and an end that ties up all the loose ends of the story. Give your story an interesting title. When you bring your story to class, you'll decorate the covers.

"After you finish your book, you'll tell about it or read it to the class. You will pass the book around so that everyone can see your illustrations."

83. Once upon a Time

Description: Help spark creativity and teach the role of plot, theme, and characters in a story by having the child create a fairy tale.

Target Skills: Writing and speaking

Things You'll Need: Children's books of fairy tales (short versions) and search engines for Internet sites with examples of fairy tales

Game Plan

1. Read a favorite fairy tale and ask the class to discuss characters, what happens in the story (plot), and the main idea or lesson in the story (theme).

2. Children will work with partners to make up their own fairy tales, keeping in mind the common elements of fairy tales.

3. Children will draw a picture illustrating the fairy tale and will practice telling their story orally.

4. Partners will present their fairy tales to the class and will take turns telling different parts of their stories. They will pass around the pictures they drew to illustrate their stories.

Sample Script: "I'm going to read you some fairy tales and then you and a partner will make up your own fairy tale to tell the class. You'll also draw a picture of a person in the fairy tale or of something that happened in the story.

"I'd like you to think about what makes fairy tales different from the other stories we read (fairy tales usually have a king, queen, or other famous person; there's usually a problem to solve; and fairy tales usually have a happy ending). After I read some, see if you can think of any other ways fairy tales are different from other stories.

"When you make up your own fairy tale, try to remember how fairy tales are different from other stories and build that into your story. You'll take turns telling your stories to the class. Maybe your story will turn out to be a little different than the one you planned. After you tell the class your fairy tale, pass around the picture you drew."

84. Frumpy Frogs, Slithery Salamanders

Description: Help the child develop creativity in language usage by using colorful words to describe familiar animals. Teach adjectives and *alliteration*, repetition of the initial consonant sound.

Target Skills: Speaking, writing (adjectives and alliteration), and vocabulary

Things You'll Need: Books with animal pictures, pen and paper

Game Plan

1. Ask the children to name animals they've seen in the neighborhood, in the zoo, and in books you've brought in. List the animals on the board.

2. Give examples of words that begin with the same initial consonant sound that the children can use to describe the animals.

3. Tell the children to work with partners. They will think of two words to describe any two animals. The describing words must begin with the same consonant sound as the animal's name.

4. Next, stage a contest to see who can give the most adjectives beginning with the same initial consonant sound as the animal's name. The last student left standing in the contest wins a small prize.

Sample Script: "You're going to tell me about animals you've seen, like pets people have and also ones you've seen in the zoo. We'll also look at pictures of animals in these books. You'll tell me the animals' names; then you and a partner will think of one or two describing words for any two of the animals.

"The describing words will begin with the same sound as the animal's name. Here are some examples: zooming zebra, giggling gorilla, cagey cat, caw caw crow. The words can be regular words like *zooming* or silly words like *caw caw*. Let your imagination go wild.

"Next we'll have a contest. You'll all line up, and the last person in the class left standing after naming the most describing words for the animals on the list wins a prize."

85. Hungry as a Hippo; Slimy as Wet Spaghetti

Description: Build descriptive ability by encouraging the child to use similes (comparisons using *like* or *as*) and encourage original thinking and avoidance of clichés (overused expressions) in writing.

Target Skills: Writing (descriptive ability and originality in language usage) and use of similes

Things You'll Need: A list of adjectives (describing words) that describe the characteristics of some other words (nouns) using *like* or *as*: for example; as silly as _____; as gentle as a _____; like a wiggly _____. Also, gather a few familiar objects such as a stuffed toy, a ball, a book, and a bowl of cereal to help children visualize the objects they're describing.

Game Plan

1. Tell the children you're going to play a word game that asks them to think of ways to describe things using *like* or *as*. Ask them to complete the similes you've made up (see Things You'll Need and Sample Script) by naming a noun for the end of the comparison.

2. Give some examples of describing words. The objects you've gathered will help you with that. You can start out by using words we commonly connect with the objects (see Sample Script).

3. Once the children understand the concept of comparing two things, suggest that they make up fresh, new comparisons that people don't often use. Listen to class examples.

4. After the children complete the comparisons, have partners make up their own comparisons using *like* or *as*. Have them make up sentences using their comparisons (see Sample Script). Add fun to the activity by using sounds and pantomime to dramatize comparisons.

Sample Script: "We're going to play a word game that asks you to compare one thing to another using the words *like* or *as*. What describing words would you say when I say, 'as _____ as a kangaroo, _____ as a whale, as _____ as a bumper car'?" (Suggested answers: jumpy, wet, jerky.)

"I'd also like you to look at the things I've brought in and think of ways to compare them using *like* or *as*." (Suggested answers: as tender *as*

121

a teddy bear, as crunchy *as* cereal.) "After we practice comparisons, I'd like you to think of some fresh, new ways to compare things. For example, instead of *wiggly as a worm*, you could say *as wiggly as wet spaghetti*. Instead of *as itchy as a bug bite*, you could say *as itchy as a pair of new pajamas*.

"For the last part of our activity I'd like you to work with a partner and make up sentences using comparisons. Use *like* or *as* to help you compare words in your sentences. For example, *I felt like a roly poly pumpkin after I ate the hot fudge sundae.* If you want, you and your partner can act out your comparison to make it more interesting."

86. **What Would You Do If . . .**

Description: Help the child verbalize thoughts about everyday problems.

Target Skills: Speaking, listening, and character development (problem solving)

Things You'll Need: Brief problem situations written ahead of time to which the child will respond, pen and paper

Game Plan

1. Have the class list at least five problem situations that have arisen or may happen at school or home. For the first few situations, you can offer ideas and have the class give opinions on the different solutions. Ask the students how they'd handle the problem.

2. Ask the children to work with partners. They will come up with their own brief problem situations to present to the class.

3. Have the partners present their problems and give their solutions to the class. See if the class can come up with more ideas.

Sample Script: "I'd like you think about what you would do if certain things happened. First we'll talk about some problems that might come up in school or at home. You'll give your ideas about how to handle each one.

"Here are some examples of problems and ways to fix them. You're having fun playing with a new toy you just got. Your brother or sister comes up and snatches it away. What do you do?" (Acceptable answers: Say, "The toy is mine. Please give it back." If the person doesn't give it back, tell a parent or adult; or say, "I'll be glad to share the toy after I've played with it awhile." Unacceptable answers: Grab the toy back from the person; tell on the person right away; or scream unkind things at the person.)

"Here is another example: Your teacher asks you to help put the toys away, but you don't feel like it." (Acceptable answer: Help clean up even though you don't feel like it because you had fun playing with the toys. Unacceptable answer: Let the other children put the toys away and go play by yourself in the book corner.)

"Here's our final example of a problem and a solution: You don't like what your parents made for dinner." (Acceptable answer: Try the food and eat a little even though it's not your favorite. Unacceptable answer: Tell your parents that you hate the food and that you're not eating dinner.)

"Next you'll work with a partner. Think of a problem that you had at home or in school and how you'd solve it. You'll tell the class about the problem and what you'd do to solve it. The class will also give their own ideas about a helpful way to handle the problem."

87. Comic Capers (Homework Helper Activity)

Description: Work on writing skills and familiarize the child with story structure and dialogue using newspaper comics.

Target Skills: Writing and speaking

Things You'll Need: Comics that have little or no dialogue from newspapers, pen, paper, construction paper, glue stick, and overhead projector

Game Plan

1. Bring in comics with bright, colorful characters but with little or no lines of dialogue that will spark children's imagination to write their own dialogues.

2. Have the children take a comic home along with construction paper. Ask the homework helper to write the dialogue for the comic that the child dictates under each segment of the comic. The dialogue should be short and should reflect the pictures and characters' gestures and expressions.

3. Children will bring the comics to class with the dialogue they've dictated. Show the children's comics on the overhead.

Sample Script: "I'm going to pass out some comics. You're going to make up your own words to fit what the people in the comics might say. Make it serious or funny. You'll take your comic home and your homework helpers will write what you tell them to include in your comic.

"You will glue your comic to the construction paper, and your helper will write the words to the comic under each picture. Be sure to draw an arrow from the comic to the words, showing which person is talking. Look at the faces of the people in the comic. Are the people happy, sad, funny, or angry? Make what they say show their feelings.

"After you finish writing your comic, you'll bring it to class, and I'll show it to everyone on the overhead projector. You or I will read the class the story you wrote."

88. How Much for the Elephant with the Missing Ear? (Homework Helper Activity)

Description: Develop critical thinking, organizational skills, and writing skills by having the child set up a store.

Target Skills: Writing, speaking, and listening

Things You'll Need: Play cash register or box with compartments; play money; small items to sell in the pretend store, such as books and small toys; tags to price items, construction paper, and markers

Game Plan

1. Set up a small store, using a toy cash register or one you've made. Use play money for currency, and ask each child to

bring in one toy or book in good condition that they no longer want. Children will place a tag on their item, listing the price. Class members will pay for the items with the play money.

2. With the help of their homework helpers, children will write short ads with construction paper and markers for the products they want to sell. On the day the child will sell the item, he or she will display the ad and tell about the item for sale.

3. The children will display their ads and talk about the items they're selling.

4. Children will take turns buying and selling items in the store. Every child will have a chance to buy one toy.

5. Over a period of days, the children will take turns buying and selling items in the store. After they have sold all the items, each child will show the item purchased and describe it to the class.

Sample Script: "We're going to play store with this toy cash register. As you can see, it has different compartments for different types of play money (change and paper money). You're going to take turns being salespeople and sell a toy or book that you no longer want that is still in good condition.

"When you go home, I'd like you to write an ad to help you sell your toy or book. Your homework helper can help you write one or two sentences about the toy you want to sell with the play money. This is called an *ad*. An ad is a commercial for a product like the ones you see in magazines.

"You'll use these tags to put a price on the toy you want to sell. When you finish selling the toy, you will put the play money in the register.

"When it's your turn to sell your toy, you'll show the class the ad you wrote and you'll have time to tell about the thing you're selling. Each person will have the chance to buy one thing." (After everyone buys a book or toy, the children will tell what they bought and describe it to the class.)

89. **Write an Animal Poem**

Description: Practice using different parts of speech by having the child compose a poem about a favorite animal.

Target Skills: Writing and speaking

Things You'll Need: Examples of nouns, adjectives, verbs, adverbs; pen; paper; poster board or butcher paper; and markers

Game Plan

1. Explain and give examples of four different parts of speech, action words (verbs), naming words (nouns), words that describe nouns (adjectives), and words that describe verbs (adverbs).

2. Tell the children to choose an animal for the subject of a short poem. They can write about one they've seen in the neighborhood or the zoo.

3. As a group, the class will compose poems about animals over a period of days. You will write on the board as they dictate. Have them revise the poem collectively after they write it.

4. You can have the students write one poem at each session for a total of five or six animal poems.

5. Write the animal poems on large poster board or butcher paper and have students illustrate each one with markers.

Sample Script: "We're going to write an animal poem together, and then I'll put it on this poster and ask three or four of you to draw the animal the way it's shown in the poem. When we finish the project, we'll have a total of six animal poems.

"To write this poem, you'll need to know four different parts of speech. You already know about action words (verbs), naming words (nouns), words that tell about nouns (adjectives), and words that tell about verbs (adverbs).

"Here are some examples of these parts of speech: The hungry monkey ate my banana. *Monkey* is a noun because it names a thing. What else can a noun name? (Answer: person or place.) *Hungry* is a describing word or adjective because it tells about the noun. Can you give me more examples of describing words? *Ate* is an action word or verb because it shows action. How many verbs can you name?

"We're also going to use adverbs in this poem. An adverb describes a verb, and it often ends in *ly*. If I say, 'The baby cried loudly,' *loudly* is an adverb because it tells how the baby cried. Here's another sentence with an adverb: 'The turtle walked slowly.' *Slowly* is an adverb because it tells how the turtle walked.

"Now that we've practiced four parts of speech, I'm going to show you how to write the animal poem. Name the animal (noun) in the first line. In the second line, write two words that describe the animal. In the third line write one action word about the animal. Add *ing* to the action word. (If the action word is *walk*, you'd make it *walking*.) In the fourth line write two adverbs that tell about the action word. Use adverbs that have *ly* in them. In the fifth and last line, think of another name for the animal. It can be more than one word."

Example of animal poem:

> Tiger
> Huge, green-eyed
> Moving
> Slowly, slyly
> Big Cat

"After you write your animal poems, I'll write them on a poster and some of you will draw pictures of the animals."

90. Create a Virtues Poster

Description: Develop speaking and writing skills by making posters about virtues the child can practice every day.

Target Skills: Speaking, writing, and character development (practicing virtues)

Things You'll Need: Poster board or butcher paper, and markers or crayons

Game Plan

1. Mention some virtues that people can practice in their lives such as kindness, courtesy, gratitude, sharing, and patience.

2. Ask the children to brainstorm ideas for putting the above-mentioned virtues into practice. Write their ideas on the board as they say them.

3. The children will work in teams of two or three to make posters representing a particular virtue. Write the name of the virtue at the top of each poster. Have the groups write or dictate different ways they can show that virtue in their everyday lives.

4. Teams will show and explain their virtue posters to the class.

5. Ask the children to report back when they've practiced any of the virtues on the posters.

Sample Script: "A virtue is doing something good for others. When we practice virtues, we feel better about ourselves, and we feel good about helping someone else. We're going to talk about some virtues. Then I'd like you to tell me ways you can show those virtues in your life.

"Here are some examples of how you can show virtues in your life: *kindness* (sharing a favorite toy with your sister or calling your grandmother); *patience* (waiting your turn, waiting for Mom or Dad to get off the phone to talk to them, and not screaming when someone makes the wrong move in a game); *thankfulness* (saying thanks for a special dinner or writing a family member a thank-you note for a gift).

"You're going to work with one or two other children to make posters about virtues. When you think about ways you can show these virtues, use the ideas we talked about and add your own. After you draw pictures showing these virtues, write or dictate ways you can show them in your lives. In a week or so, I'll ask if anyone had a chance to practice the virtue. Tell us how you felt and how you think the other person felt when you practiced the virtue.

"You're also going to tell the class about your virtue posters. Choose one student from your group to show the poster and one to explain the poster."

91. Tell a Tall Tale (Homework Helper Activity)

Description: Polish storytelling, listening, and speaking skills as the child creates tall tales.

Target Skills: Speaking and listening

Things You'll Need: Short, humorous tall tales (found in a search engine for children on the Internet under *tall tales* or in a children's book of tall tales)

Game Plan

1. Look up some tall tales or campfire stories suitable for young children in a search engine or a children's book, and read some to the class. Explain that all tall tales have certain things in common, and review those elements.

2. With the help of their homework helpers, the children will invent their own tall tales following the conventions of the tall tale story.

3. The class will tell how the tall tales are different from the stories they usually hear. The children will read or tell their tall tales to the class.

Sample Script: "We're going to learn about tall tales today. Many years ago in our country, people told tall tales to entertain one another. Back in the olden days, there were no movies or TV, so telling stories was a favorite thing for people to do during their free time.

"Listen to the stories I tell you and see if you can tell me why they're tall tales. The characters in a tall tale are bigger than real people. As you'll see when I read the story, wild, out of the ordinary things happen in a tall tale, things you don't usually see in other stories we read.

"Think about what you want your tall tale to be about, then write or dictate your story to your homework helper. Make it short, and make it funny if you want. Then bring it in to read or tell the class."

92. Brainstorm a Poem (Homework Helper Activity)

Description: Develop an understanding of rhyme in poetry by having the child brainstorm rhyming words and write a poem using the words.

Target Skills: Writing, speaking, and listening

Things You'll Need: Pen and paper

Game Plan

1. Have the class brainstorm a list of one- or two-syllable rhyming words in preparation for writing short poems. Provide a list of these rhyming words to the homework helpers.

2. Ask the students to choose three or four sets of rhyming words from the list or to use some of their own rhyming words when writing poems with their helpers.

3. Children will write or dictate three- or four-line poems with their helpers' assistance using the sets of rhyming words. The lines can rhyme at the end or in the middle of the line.

4. Students or their helpers will write the final draft of the poem on good paper, and the student will draw a picture in keeping with the poem's theme.

5. Students will bring their poems to class to read (or for you to read).

Sample Script: "Think of some words that rhyme. I'll write them on the board as you say them. Here are some examples of rhyming words: *cat, scat, hat; mouse, house; cheese, please.* Here is a poem that rhymes using the words. Notice that some of the words rhyme in the middle and at the end of the line and some words rhyme only at the end of the line. When you write your poem, you can rhyme the words either way.

> I told the *cat* to *scat*.
> She ran after a *mouse*
> hiding under the *house*.

Here is another poem with rhyming words:

> Would you like to *play*?
> It's a sunny *day*.
> We can bake a *cake*
> and eat it on the *lake*.

Your homework helper will help you write a poem like the sample poems, using three or four pairs of rhyming words from the list we made and from ones you think of.

"After you make up your poem, you or your helper will write it on paper. Draw a picture of what the poem is about. You will bring in your poems to read to the class."

93. Build a Silly, Scary Creature

Description: Reinforce imaginative thinking and writing skills by asking the child to invent a creature.

Target Skills: Writing, speaking, and listening

Things You'll Need: Pen, paper, markers, and poster paper

Game Plan

1. Ask the children what a silly, scary creature would look like to them. Write ideas on the board and discuss. Provide prompts to help the children visualize the different types of creatures they can write about.

2. The children will work with a partner to draw pictures of their creatures. They will make up names for their creatures and

131

write or dictate one- or two-sentence descriptions of the creatures.

3. After they complete the drawings and descriptions, the children will show their drawings to the class and tell a brief story about the creature.

Sample Script: "How would you like to make up a story about a silly, scary creature? First, we're going to write some ideas on the board and talk about how such a creature might look. Here are some questions to get you started. When you write about the creature, I'd like you to answer the questions in sentences. What would the creature's face (eyes, nose, mouth, hair) look like? What would his or her voice sound like? Maybe you can say a few words sounding like you're the creature. How would the creature's body look? How would the creature move? How would it try to scare people, and how would it act silly?

"After we talk about how a silly, scary creature might look, I'd like you and a partner to invent your own creature. You can write or tell me about your creature in a couple of sentences. Draw a picture of the creature and we'll write the sentences under the picture. Make up a short, short story to tell about your silly, scary creature. You'll tell your story and show your picture to the class."

94. Noun and Verb-a-Thon

Description: Teach parts of speech by playing a fast-paced game. Write sentences using nouns and verbs.

Target Skills: Writing, speaking, and sentence structure

Things You'll Need: Pen, paper, and timer

Game Plan

1. Review the meaning and give examples of nouns (naming words) and verbs (action words).

2. Have students give examples of nouns and verbs and write them on the board or on poster board to display.

3. For the contest, the children take turns naming nouns and then verbs. The last one remaining in the game wins. If you want, assign a time limit for naming the nouns and verbs. Add the nouns and verbs the children list to the poster.

4. After the game is over, ask the class to compose sentences using the nouns and verbs you've posted. Write the sentences on the board or on a poster. Students will take turns identifying the nouns and verbs after you write and read each sentence. Then they can underline the nouns and circle the verbs, or you direct them to do it.

Sample Script: "Nouns are naming words. They name persons, places, or things. Verbs show action. *Benjamin Franklin* is a noun because he was a person. *Disneyland* is a noun because it is a place. *Blocks*, *cars*, and *bubbles* are all nouns because they are things. *Sing*, *run*, and *smile* are verbs because they show action.

"Now I'd like you to tell me some nouns and verbs. Think of the people, places, and things you see every day. These are nouns. Think of the things you do every day. These are verbs. I'll write them on this poster, and later you'll make up sentences using them.

"We're also going to play a game using nouns and verbs. First, everyone will take a turn naming nouns; then everyone will take a turn naming verbs. The last person to stay in the game wins. Everyone can play this game because everyone can name at least two or three nouns and verbs.

"Next, you're going to write sentences using the nouns and verbs on our list and some that you thought of in the game. Remember that a sentence needs a complete thought. It has to make good sense when you say it.

"Why is *The Ferris wheel* not a sentence?" (It's part of a sentence because it doesn't make sense by itself. You need to add more words.) "Why is *The Ferris wheel soared to the sky* a sentence?" (It makes sense and everyone knows what you're talking about when you say it.)

"I'll write the sentences with nouns and verbs on this poster. I'll ask you to take turns telling me the nouns and verbs in each sentence. Then we'll underline the nouns and circle the verbs in each sentence."

95. In with Sentences! Out with Fragments!

Description: Give practice in differentiating sentences from fragments by engaging the child in a fast-paced game.

Target Skills: Writing (sentences versus fragments), reading, speaking, and listening

Things You'll Need: Prewritten information (five sentences and five sentence fragments in jumbled order), two signs (one with a plus sign and the other with a minus), and poster board and marker or chalkboard

Game Plan

1. Review the meaning of a sentence versus a fragment. Write examples and explain the difference between the two. A sentence gives a complete thought that makes sense and can stand by itself. A fragment is a part of a sentence that cannot stand alone.

2. Distribute the plus and minus signs. Display and read the five sentences and five sentence fragments. Have students hold up signs (plus for sentences and minus for fragments) as you read and display each group of words. Discuss any questions that come up.

3. Ask the students to turn all the fragments into sentences. Ask why they are now sentences (Suggested answer: They are sentences because they make sense and give a complete thought).

Sample Script: "Let's talk about the difference between a sentence and a part of a sentence. A part of a sentence is called a *sentence fragment*. It does not make sense and cannot stand by itself. We want to write sentences, not fragments, because sentences make sense.

"Here are some examples of sentence fragments. Try to turn the fragments or pieces of sentences into sentences." (Examples: 1. Fragment: *at the circus*; Sentence: *We saw dancing polar bears at the circus.* 2. Fragment: *leap three feet*; Sentence: *My cat can leap three feet.*)

"I'm going to give you a plus sign and a minus sign. I've written some fragments and sentences on this poster. When I read and show you a fragment, hold up the minus sign. When I read and show you a sentence, hold up the plus sign. If you're not sure of your answers or have any questions about sentences and sentence fragments, we'll talk about it.

"Now that you've voted on the sentences and sentence fragments, I'd like you to turn the fragments into sentences. Let the class know why they are now sentences."

96. Dear Cousin, Aunt, Uncle, or Grandparent (Homework Helper Activity)

Description: Resurrect the lost art of letter writing by having the child write a friendly letter to a relative. Give writing practice while stressing courtesy and social skills.

Target Skills: Writing, following directions, and character development (family closeness)

Things You'll Need: Copies of template for friendly letter based on student survey about content, and pens

Game Plan

1. Explain that before computers were invented and people e-mailed one another, people wrote friendly letters to each other.

2. Ask the class what types of things they might want to say in a friendly letter to a relative. Tell them to think of a family member to whom they'd like to write. Send a letter template home to a homework helper. If children would rather write a letter using original ideas instead of the template, encourage them to do so.

3. Using the template as a guideline or using their own ideas, students will write or dictate their letters to the helpers. The students will stamp and mail the letters.

4. As return letters come in from family members, ask students to report to the class about some of the things their relatives wrote about in their letters.

Sample Script: "Before e-mail, people wrote friendly letters to family or friends. Writing letters gave them a chance to tell others what they were doing and to find out what was new with the other person. It's fun to write a friendly letter, and you're going to start writing one today with your homework helper.

"Think of a family member you'd like to write to, someone you don't see every day. I'll give you a paper, called a *template*, to help you write a friendly letter. If you want, you can think of your own ideas to write about in your letter.

"Dictate the letter to your homework helper. Then you can stamp your letter and mail it. When the person writes back, you can tell the class some interesting things about the letter and your family member.

"Here is the template to help you write your friendly letter":

Dear _____,

I'm writing this letter to tell you _____

_____

_____.

    What have you been doing lately?
    Here's something new I've learned: _____

_____

_____.

    I've also been having fun with my friends _____ and
_____. When we get together we like to _____

_____.

    Please write back to me and tell me how you are. I miss you and hope to see you soon.

    Your cousin (or whatever you want to call yourself to the person you write to),

_____

9️7️. Plot a Story

Description: Teach the concept of plot in a story. Help build reading comprehension and critical thinking skills by discussing what happens in the beginning, middle, and end of a story.

Target Skills: Reading and speaking

Things You'll Need: Picture storybook or chapter book with a clearly defined plot

Game Plan

1. Explain the word *plot* (what the story is about). Say that every plot has a beginning, middle, and end. Ask the children to tell you the plot of a story they've recently read at home or in school.

2. Read a picture storybook (longer picture book with a more complex plot) or a chapter book to the class.

3. Ask the students to tell you the beginning, middle, and end of the story you read aloud to them. If necessary, ask them leading questions to help them differentiate one part of the story from another.

4. After they've given a summary of the plot, ask them to tell which part of the story they liked best and why.

5. Ask the class if they would change any part of the story. If so, how would they change it?

Sample Script: "The plot of a story is what happens in the story. Every story has three parts: the beginning, middle, and end. In the beginning we meet the characters and find out what the story is about. What is the problem the character has to solve? Maybe the person is going on an adventure. Where is the character going, and what does he or she plan to do?

"The middle of the story tells us more about what's going to happen to the main character. It goes deeper into the problem or it takes us further into the person's adventure.

"The end of the story tells us how everything turns out. What happened to the main character by the end of the story?

"After I read the story, I'd like you to tell me what happens in the beginning, middle, and end of the story. Then I'll ask you what part of the story you liked best and why. If you were the author, if you'd change any part of the story, what part would it be and why?"

98. What Does a Book Teach?

Description: Help the child understand theme in a story and enhance reading for meaning by discussing theme, the main point a story makes.

Target Skills: Reading, writing, speaking, and character development (learning universal truths through literature)

Things You'll Need: Picture storybook or chapter book that has a clearly defined theme or fables for children

Game Plan

1. Discuss what we mean by the plot, what happens in a story. Ask the students to talk briefly about the plot of a favorite book they've read.

2. Tell the students that every story has a theme or a main idea. Sometimes the theme teaches something. The theme of a story always gives us something to think about. The plot tells what happens, and the theme tells why the author wrote the story.

3. Before reading a story or fable, ask the children to think about the theme, what they learned from reading the story. They should be able to state the theme in one sentence. Point out that it takes more sentences to write or talk about the plot because the plot is telling the whole story in our own words.

4. Ask the students to work with a partner and to state the theme of the story you read. Write the various themes they tell you on the board and discuss all of them, explaining why certain ones are the best statements of the story's theme.

Sample Script: "We've talked about plot, the things that happen in a story. Every story has a main character and a beginning, middle, and end. Who would like to tell us the plot of a story we've read?

"You can see that it takes time to tell the plot of a story. You can't give the plot in one or two sentences. But the stories we read have something else called the *theme*. The theme of the story is the lesson in the story, what we learn by reading the story.

"Here are some examples of how you can say some story themes: It pays to be patient; telling the truth is always better than lying; it's good to treat others the same way we want to be treated; stay with something that's hard to do, and you'll win in the end; or it's important not to give up.

"You can say all of these themes in one sentence. I'm going to read you a story, and I'll give you and your partner time to think about the theme. Then I'll write your ideas on the board, and we'll decide which is the best way to say the theme of the story."

99. Characters Come Alive (Homework Helper Activity)

Description: Examine characterization in a favorite story. Talk about how the author brings characters to life and makes them memorable.

Target Skills: Reading, writing, and speaking

Things You'll Need: Picture storybook or chapter book, e-mail access at home or children can correspond with a partner by writing notes

Game Plan

1. Now that the children have gained an understanding of plot and theme, you can discuss characters. Talk about how the author makes the characters in a story come alive. Use guiding

questions to help the students learn about characters. Ask them to think of their own questions to ask to learn more about characters.

2. Read a story and ask the children to consider the main and supporting characters. See what insights they come up with about the characters, using your questions and theirs as a guideline.

3. As a follow-up, ask partners to pretend they're two characters in the story. As a home project with the assistance of their homework helpers, students will write an e-mail from one character to another about any topics they choose from the story. They will try to speak and act the way the characters in the story do. If one or both of the partners do not have e-mail access, they can dictate or write notes to each other as the characters in the story.

4. Students will bring in copies of their e-mails or notes and read or ad-lib their dialogues.

Sample Script: "We've learned about plot, what happens in a story, and theme, the lesson in the story. Now we're going to talk about the characters, the people in the story. Who can tell me how we learn about characters?" (Suggested answers: How they look, what they say to other characters, what they're thinking, what they do.)

"When I read a story today, I'd like you to think about the people in the story. Here are some questions to think about: What does the character look like? How old is he or she? What kinds of things is the character interested in? How does the character act? What kinds of things does the character say to other people? How does the character deal with problems? What did you like about the character? If you were the author, would you change anything about the character?

"After we talk about the characters in the story, I'm going to ask you and a partner to pretend you're two of the characters in the story and to send each other an e-mail, acting like the characters would. You can talk about anything as long as it deals with what happened in the story. Your homework helpers can help you write to each other.

"You and your partner will bring in a copy of your e-mails or the notes you wrote to one another as the characters in the story. You or I will read what you said. You can also use your own words to tell what you said about the characters in the story."

100. Today Is a New Day (Homework Helper Activity)

Description: Write sentences in a journal stressing positive thinking in response to prompts about the day's activities.

Target Skills: Writing, speaking, and character development (gratitude, optimism)

Things You'll Need: Prepared prompts for writing, journals, and pen

Game Plan

1. Tell the children that a journal helps them think about what they did each day. Keeping a journal will help them think about the good things in their lives.

2. With the assistance of the homework helper, the children will write or dictate short journal entries twice a week for the next three weeks.

3. Distribute the prompts for journal writing. Tell the children that they will answer each question in one or two complete sentences. They will answer at least three questions every time they write.

4. At the end of the three weeks, the children will choose their best journal entry and read or tell it to the class.

Sample Script: "Many people enjoy writing in a journal because they like to think about what they did each day. You're going to write a journal about good things that happen in your life, things that make you happy and thankful.

"I'm going to give you a list of questions called *prompts*. I'd like you to answer the questions in one or two complete sentences. You will write in your journal twice a week for the next three weeks. Use different questions every time you write, and answer at least three questions.

"Your homework helper will help you write the answers to the journal questions. After you write in your journal for three weeks, you will choose your best journal entry and bring it in to read or tell the class.

"Here are the journal questions:

1. What did you enjoy doing today?

2. What did you learn today?

3. Who did you enjoy seeing today?

4. Name one thing you are thankful for today and tell why.

5. Tell about something kind someone did for you today or another time.

6. What can you do to help someone have a happy day?"

101. Question and Answer Book (Homework Helper Activity)

Description: Teach descriptive writing skills and punctuation (periods and question marks) by having the child write his or her own life story in response to questions.

Target Skills: Writing (answering questions, descriptive skills), punctuation, and critical thinking

Things You'll Need: Drawing materials, pen, notebook for each child, and prepared questions

Game Plan

1. The child will compose a seven-page question and answer book using questions you provide to the child and the homework helper.

2. The homework helper will write one question at the top of each page and with the helper's assistance, the child will answer each question in two or three sentences. The child will illustrate each page with an appropriate drawing.

3. Explain the use of periods and question marks in writing. A period ends a sentence that tells us something. A question mark ends a sentence that asks a question. The students will use periods in answering the questions at the top of each page. They will use question marks in the final activity that follows the question and answer book.

4. They will circle all periods and question marks in their sentences.

5. At the end of the week, the children will bring their question and answer books to class. Call on a student and tell the student to answer a question from one to seven. Then that student will call on another student and give the student a number from one to seven.

6. The students will continue asking and answering questions until all the students have had a chance to read their answers. Then students will take turns asking another child the question, "[Write a question to ask a friend.]"

Sample Script: "Today you're going to start writing a question and answer book. It will be your very own book with one question at the top of each page. At the end of the book, you'll have a chance to ask someone in the class a question.

"You're going to write this book with your homework helper and then bring it to class at the end of the week. Everyone will have a chance to give a number and ask someone to answer the question they wrote for that number.

"I'd like you to write or dictate your answers in sentences (one to three sentences to a question). Think about what type of punctuation marks to use. Sentences that tell us something end with a period. Sentences that ask a question end with a question mark. Circle all the periods and question marks in your answers.

"Here are the questions you'll work on with your helper:

1. What is your favorite toy or game, and why do you feel that way?

2. Describe one of your best friends and tell why you like being with this friend.

3. How many people are in your family? What are their names?

4. What do you like to do best with your family?

5. What is your favorite book? Why?

6. What is your favorite dinner and dessert?

7. What makes you happy?

After you finish answering the questions, you will write two questions of your own for people to answer:

1. Write a question to ask your mother, father, or guardian.

2. Write a question to ask a friend.

After you read or tell one of your answers from your book in class, you will ask another child to answer the question, '[Write a question to ask a friend.]'"